Media Literacy

Activities for Understanding the Scripted World

Roberta Solomon Endich

Linworth
PUBLISHING, INC

**Your Trusted
Library-to-Classroom Connection.**
Books, Magazines, and Online

Published by Linworth Publishing, Inc.
480 East Wilson Bridge Road, Suite L
Worthington, Ohio 43085

Copyright © 2004 by Linworth Publishing, Inc.

ISBN 1-58683-094-5

5 4 3 2 1

Table of Contents

Table of Contents cont.

Table of Contents cont.

Table of Contents cont.

About the Author

Roberta Solomon Endich is a library media specialist at the M.E. Small Elementary School, one of the eight schools in the Dennis-Yarmouth Regional School District on Cape Cod, Massachusetts. There she applies a unique blend of abilities in teaching library and research skills and media literacy to students in grades K–5. Her position affords her the opportunity to awaken children's interests and intellectual curiosity by helping them discover the myriad of fiction and nonfiction resources available in print and online and how to use them to obtain accurate and authoritative information.

Ms. Endich is a graduate of Kean University in New Jersey and received her M.Ed. in Library Media Services from Bridgewater State College in Massachusetts. She began her teaching career in the 1970s teaching high school English in New Jersey and then left the teaching profession for the allure of Cape Cod and a stint at operating her own retail business. Ms. Endich returned to the academic community and currently lives on Cape Cod with her two children, Tamara and David, and their two dogs, Rainbow and Sunshine.

This is her second book for Linworth Books.

Acknowledgments

I would like to thank Kathy Schrock who invited and encouraged me to write another manuscript, patiently dealing with my struggle to meet deadlines.

Thank you to the kind librarians at the Truro Public Library for handling my many book requests from other libraries with a smile.

Thank you to my hundreds of students who wondered why I kept asking them questions about how they spent their free time and how much TV they watched. I was sad and amazed to discover that many of their most precious possessions were their video games and computers.

A special thank you to my children, David and Tamara, who put up with their moody Mom during my intense work sessions, often making dinner and seeing that I was well nourished and then tip-toeing around the house so they wouldn't disturb me.

Tamara and David, please accept my apologies, but I am truly convinced that spending time without electronics (yes, even my computer) is the best way to develop your incredibly creative, imaginative, artistic, and inquisitive minds. Remember, the Buddha says: "There is only one time when it is essential to awaken. That time is now."

How to Use This Book

American schoolchildren spend more time watching television and playing video and computer games than they do attending school or at play. Because of the incredible amount of time they spend viewing a world that is scripted for them, they need to develop the skills that will help them to analyze what they see. The media shapes our visions of ourselves, or rather, how we are "supposed" to look and act. It presents views of families, gender, aging, and violence in a way that is meant to influence our beliefs. Is what the media presents true or do we need to question these views?

As a library media specialist and parent of two children, I am very aware of the divided reality most children toggle every day. They have the virtual world in which they play, and the real world in which they live. How can they learn to discriminate between the two and decide what to believe? How does the media shape a child's perception of the world? Who controls and creates the messages?

About the Book

Media literacy is a literacy beyond reading and writing that includes the ability to read messages through visual images. This book is a collection of 182 activities designed to help develop and refine student perception of this scripted world. The cross-curricular, McREL standards-based activities cover some electronic media (radio, television, video games, and photography) and print media (newspapers, magazines, books, advertisements, junk mail, travel brochures, and billboards). Advertising, target audience, bias, and sales are all touched upon in the units. There are no activities for the Internet and evaluating Web sites, as there are already many excellent activity books available for teachers.

The activities are intended to help children develop higher levels of critical thinking; to help them discriminate between fiction and nonfiction; to detect the persuasive intent of what they see; and to learn about the economic and political functions, and relationships, of media. The activities will help them learn to gather information, analyze the construction of the message, evaluate the content to determine if it expresses their own views or someone else's, detect bias, and create their own messages through the various types of media explored.

The activities can be integrated into many different curriculum units. Language arts, math, technology, science, and art are all incorporated into many of the activities. A group of activities called Literature Connections are based on children's books that present scenarios demonstrating the huge impact media plays in children's lives.

The book begins with general classroom activities, such as a word wall and a glossary, that help prepare students for each selected unit. Full-page reproducibles assist students in their analysis of information. In addition, some activities help students create their own media messages. Production of advertisements, newspapers, and other scripted materials will allow them to understand how everything they read and see from the media is carefully and critically planned. Technology standards and benchmarks are infused into many of the activities. Software programs that incorporate digital imaging are also valuable assets to teaching media literacy.

The book is designed in a way that will allow easy selection of appropriate activities for each grade level and type of media. Use of these activities will help media-saturated children understand what they are watching on TV, listening to on the radio, and seeing at the movie theaters; and why they are spending millions of dollars on heavily advertised clothing, food, and entertainment. The activities will hopefully assist them in becoming more sophisticated and savvy consumers of media and goods.

Activity 1 — Classroom Collection and Preparation

Grade levels: 4–8

Activity description: Provide visual examples of the many kinds of media we encounter on a regular basis.

Preparation and materials:
Collect various types of "media" to display as students develop their ideas of media literacy. These might include newspapers, magazines, books, tapes, CDs, computer programs (various formats), a print-out from the Internet, a television (you might use a *TV Guide*), a radio, and anything else that is accessible and appropriate.

Activity 2 — A Personal Student Media Literacy Glossary

Grade levels: 4–8

Standards: Language Arts, Research Skills

Activity description: Students will create and organize a space to record new words and definitions in the area of media literacy.

Preparation and materials:
Assemble dictionaries and notebooks for each student.

Procedure:

- Give each student a small notebook in which to create and keep his or her Media Literacy Glossary.

- As the classroom activities proceed, have students enter new words.

- Students will look up unfamiliar words in the dictionary and record the definitions.

- Students will share their words and definitions on a regular basis.

Evaluation: Students will expand their vocabularies and create their own subject glossaries.

My Media Literacy Glossary

Activity 3   A Personal Computer-Generated Glossary

Grade levels: 4–8

Standards: Language Arts, Technology

Activity description: Students will use a word processing program like Microsoft® Word® or a database like Microsoft® Access® to create a personal computerized media literacy glossary.

Preparation and materials:
- Make sure students are familiar with the application of your choice.

Procedure:
- Microsoft Word
    - ▶ Create a new Blank Document.
    - ▶ Select Table from the menu bar.
    - ▶ Select Insert > Table.
    - ▶ Create with 2 columns and 20 rows (these can be adjusted at any time) and select Auto Fit to contents.

- Microsoft Access
    - ▶ Create new Blank Access Database.
    - ▶ Name the file Glossary.
    - ▶ Select Create table by entering data.
    - ▶ Right click on Field 1, select Rename Column and name it "Word."
    - ▶ Right click on Field 2, select Rename Column and name it "Definition."

- As the Media Literacy unit develops, students will add new words and their definitions to their electronic journals.

- At the end of the unit, both applications can alphabetize (sort) the entries.

Evaluation: Students will demonstrate their ability to create a database and manipulate basic data and/or create a table.

Related Internet Resources:
Florida Gulf Coast University. Word 2000 Tutorial — Tables. 2002. 18 October 2003. <http://www.fgcu.edu/support/office2000/word/tables.html>

Strykler, John. ExcelHelp. Bay City Schools. 18 October 2003. <http://www.bcschools.net/staff/AccessHelp.htm>

Grade levels: 4–8

Standard: Language Arts

Activity description: Select a location in the classroom or hall nearby and call it the "Media Literacy Word Wall."

Preparation and materials:
- Use pre-cut, or create your own, oak tag strips 9" x 3".

Procedure:
- Add new words to the wall after each lesson. This can be done by handwriting the words on the oak tag strips or using a word processing program to type each word in an extra-large font (e.g., 120 point). Print and cut out the words, glue them to strips, laminate, and put them on the word wall.

- Use new additions to the word wall as a vocabulary assignment each week.

- Make sure students practice and recognize the words and use them correctly.

- Student vocabulary will increase and incorporate new media literacy words.

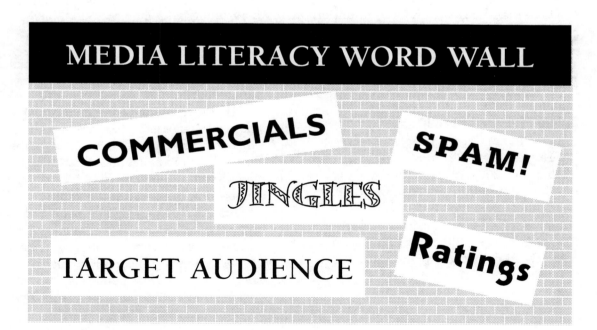

MEDIA LITERACY WORD WALL

COMMERCIALS

SPAM!

JINGLES

Ratings

TARGET AUDIENCE

Grade levels: 4–8

Standards: Visual Arts, Language Arts, Thinking and Reasoning

Activity description: Students will brainstorm and develop a definition of the term "media literacy."

Preparation and materials:

- Chalkboard or whiteboard
- Examples of various media (see Activity 1)

Procedure:

- Students are probably familiar with the term "literacy." Query them and get their ideas.

- Ask them to describe various "media" they encounter on a regular basis. The answers will vary according to age and sophistication.

  ▸ You should guide them to include as many of these as possible:
  - Advertisements
  - Billboards
  - Books
  - CDs (music)
  - Comics
  - Computer
  - Junk mail
  - Newspapers
  - Photography and cameras
  - Posters
  - Radio
  - Sides of trucks and buses
  - T-shirts
  - Telephone
  - Television
  - Travel brochures
  - Video games
  - Web sites

- Have them brainstorm for a definition of "media literacy."

- As they answer, record their answers.

Evaluation: Students will understand the basic elements of media literacy.

Related Internet Resources:

Rogers, Susan Freas. *What is Media Literacy?* Media Literacy.com. 18 October 2003. <http://www.medialiteracy.com/whatismlpage.htm>

Alliance for a Media Literate America. *Media Literacy.* 18 October 2003. <http://www.nmec.org/medialit.html>

NOTE: In 2001, the Alliance for a Media Literate America (AMLA) chose this definition: *"Media literacy empowers people to be both critical thinkers and creative producers of an increasingly wide range of messages using image, language, and sound. It is the skillful application of literacy skills to media and technology messages. As communication technologies transform society, they impact our understanding of ourselves, our communities, and our diverse cultures, making media literacy an essential life skill for the 21st century."*

Grade levels: 4–8

Standards: Language Arts, Viewing, Thinking and Reasoning

Activity description: Students will brainstorm to generate categories for media messages.

Preparation and materials:

- Whiteboard or chalkboard to record student responses
- Samples of different types of media

Procedure:

- Explain to students that media can be broken up into four categories:
  - ▶ One-to-one communication
  - ▶ Entertainment
  - ▶ Information to a large group of people
  - ▶ Persuasion

- Students will brainstorm, naming various types of media, and try to place them in the above categories. Some media messages might belong to more than one group.

- Examples might be:
  - ▶ One-to-one communication
    - Letter
    - Telephone
    - E-mail
  - ▶ Entertainment
    - Television shows
    - Video games
    - Movies
  - ▶ Information to a large group of people
    - News programs
    - Newspapers
    - Internet
  - ▶ Persuasion
    - Advertising
    - Direct Marketing (junk mail)
    - Telemarketing

Evaluation: Students will recognize there are specific ways and reasons in the scripting and delivery of media messages.

Standards: Language Arts, Thinking and Reasoning

Grade levels: 4–8

Activity description: Discuss what is meant by "scripted." Relate this to the media that were selected in Activity #5.

Preparation and materials:
- Whiteboard or chalkboard to record connections

Procedure:
- Ask students to define the word "scripted."
  - ▸ Be sure to add this into their glossary and onto the word wall!
- Take one of the media messages (e.g., a magazine advertisement) and ask the students if they think someone wrote it for a particular reason, to whom they think it was directed, and why it was written the way it was.
- For older students, you might let them examine a newspaper article and answer the same questions. You might find two newspapers that cover the same story differently.
- One by one, have students examine a medium and describe how they think a particular media message is scripted.

Evaluation: Students will acknowledge that all media is scripted.

Related Internet Resources:
Dictionary.com. *Scripted.* 2002. 17 October 2003.
<http://www.dictionary.com/search?q=scripted>

NOTE: This is a stunning example of how we (the audience) are given information. At first it may seem unbelievable to the students. The next set of activities will provide them with more assessment tools.

Grade levels: 4–8

Standards: Visual Arts, Language Arts, Thinking and Reasoning

Activity description: Students will determine the source of specific media.

Preparation and materials:
- Collect several types of media. Include magazine ads, newspaper ads, junk mail, and flyers.
- Display these media products for the class to examine.

Procedure:
Students will examine each type of media and answer the questions:
- Who created this?
- Why was the media created?
- Who will it benefit?
- How will they benefit?

Evaluation: Students will begin to realize that most media messages are directed to create financial gain for someone or a group (corporation).

Grade levels: 4–8

Standards: Visual Arts, Mathematics, Language Arts

Activity description: Students are introduced to media economics.

Preparation and materials:

- Collect some financial statistics about advertising.

- Create questions for your students to answer (or guess). Here are some examples:
  - How many media messages are we exposed to (on average) each day?
    - 3000
  - How much do companies spend on advertising to each person in a year?
    - $500
  - How much does it cost to put a 30-second ad in a prime-time network television show?
    - Average cost is $180,000.
    - A 30-second spot on *Friends* averages $455,700, according to *Advertising Age's* annual prime-time network pricing survey.
  - What magazine makes the most money?
    - *TV Guide*
  - How many companies own 80% of the radio stations in the United States?
    - 4
  - How many different ads does McDonald's create in a single year?
    - 1,000

Procedure:

- Begin the lesson by asking students to think about the messages they've already seen or heard that day. Break it down into type of media. By the time a child goes to school, they may have been exposed to:
  - TV
  - Radio
  - World Wide Web
  - Billboards and signs

- Proceed with the questions prepared in the above section, and see if students can even guess any of the answers.
  - Ask them which of the answers was the most surprising?
  - Which question got the largest variety of answers?

Evaluation: Students will understand the financial cost of creating media messages.

Related Internet Resources:

You can download a .pdf of the complete *Ad Age* TV Ad Price Chart from this site. AdAge.com. 2002. Crain Communications Inc. 16 October 2003. <http://www.adage.com>

Channel One Teacher.com. *Who pays for Mass Media?* 16 October 2003. <http://www.teachworld.com/tw_pages/teach_adv_lesson1.html>

Grade levels: 4–8

Standards: Behavioral Studies, Visual Arts

Activity description: By attaching common perceptions (stereotypes) to breeds of dogs, students will be able to understand how they might develop misconceptions about the qualities of a real animal.

Preparation and materials:

- Get pictures of common breeds of dogs.
    - Use the Google® search engine at <http://www.google.com>; select the tab for "images" and type in the breed for a varied selection of photos.
    - Petnet.com at <http://www.petnet.com.au/dogs/dogbreedindex.html> has breeds in alphabetical order and each brings up a photo.
- Display the pictures around the room.
    - Have the breed name on an oak tag strip that is not attached to the picture.
    - Have a blank sheet of paper attached to the bottom of each photo where you will later write the qualities of the dogs.

Procedure:

- Have students identify breeds that are familiar to them.
    - Students will match breed names to photos.
- When breeds are identified, have students name some qualities of each animal.
- Write these qualities under the photo of each dog.
- Stop and have the class think about a quality that might be a stereotype.
    - Pit bulls are vicious.
    - Poodles are yappy.
    - Dachshunds are mean.
    - Cairn terriers are biters.
    - Beagles are dumb.
- Do students know any dogs of these (or other) breeds that do NOT fit the stereotype?
- How can this apply to people considering race and cultural differences?

Evaluation: Students will demonstrate how easy it is to stereotype and realize it is not valid to define a particular dog, person, or culture in that way.

Related Internet Resources:

Petnet.com. *Dog Breeds.* 17 October 2003.
<http://www.petnet.com.au/dogs/dogbreedindex.html>

Dog Breed Info Center. *Alphabetical Order.* 1999–2002. 17 October 2003.
<http://www.dogbreedinfo.com/abc.htm>

The Barking Lot. *Traits.* 1997–2002. 17 October 2003.
<http://www.barkinglot.com/traits.html>

Grade levels: 4–8

Standards: Thinking and Reasoning, Language Arts, Visual Arts

Activity description: Students will explore some examples of bias.

Preparation and materials:
- Whiteboard or chalkboard

Procedure:
- Students will define bias. Be sure they add this to their glossaries.
  - ▸ Bias in a media message means that it is influenced by the attitudes and background of its interviewers, writers, photographers, and editors.
  - ▸ The seven violations or indications of bias are:
    1. Misleading definitions and terminology
    2. Imbalanced reporting
    3. Opinions disguised as news
    4. Lack of context
    5. Selective omission
    6. Using true facts to draw false conclusions
    7. Distorting facts

- Students will brainstorm to determine the different types of bias they might encounter in media messages. They should include:
  - ▸ Family portrayal in programs and advertising
    - • Does family portrayal change with race?
  - ▸ Are certain products like alcohol or tobacco targeted to specific groups?
  - ▸ Is there gender bias in programs and advertising?
    - • Define gender bias.
  - ▸ How is the female body portrayed in ads?
  - ▸ How are medicines portrayed?
  - ▸ Can you believe food ads?

Evaluation: Students will be able to understand the bias in media messages.

Related Internet Resources:
FAIR. *Fairness and Accuracy in Reporting. How to Detect Bias in News Media.* 2002. 17 October 2003. <http://www.fair.org/activism/detect.html>

Honest Reporting.com. *What is Bias?* 2002. 17 October 2003. <http://www.honestreporting.com/a/What_is_Bias.asp>

Grade levels: 4–8

Standards: Behavioral Studies

Activity description: Introduce students to the concept of cultural stereotyping.

Preparation and materials:
- Chalkboard or whiteboard

Procedure:
- Ask students to think of their favorite thing.
- Have them draw a picture of it.
  - ▶ They will keep these saved (and undisclosed) for later discussion.
- Ask the students to imagine someone from another culture.
  - ▶ Ask students to think of what the other person might think of as his or her favorite thing.
  - ▶ Record what "our" culture's child might list in a column next to what a child of the "other" culture might want.
    - Are the favorite things similar or different?
    - Are any of the favorite things good choices for either culture?
- Have students reveal their original "favorite thing."
  - ▶ Would this fit his or her interpretation of something that someone in another culture might pick?
- Discuss the importance of individual tastes and differences.

Evaluation: Students will develop an understanding of how people stereotype others and be able to identify their own perceptions of various stereotypes.

Grade levels: 4–8

Standards: Visual Arts, Thinking and Reasoning, Language Arts

Activity description: Students will determine what they consider to be advertising by talking about the variety of messages they receive during a day.

Preparation and materials:
- Students will be assigned to keep track of the number of ads they see and hear in a given day. These should include billboards, signs, posted flyers, and even logos on clothing.

Procedure:
- Using the student findings, discuss with the students what they think is advertising and what is not.
- Be sure to include product logos on clothing, school equipment, and even on school supplies.

Evaluation: Students will come up with their class definition of what to include in the term "advertising."

ADVERTISING RECORD WORKSHEET

Name: _____

Directions: Notice the ads that you see while you travel to and from school, wherever you go after school and while you are at home tonight. Fill out the chart below as best you can.

Where did you see the ad?	What is the ad for?	Do you use the product?

Grade levels: 4–8

Standards: Visual Arts, Behavioral Arts, Language Arts, Working Together

Activity description: The class will break down the separate components of media literacy and try to understand them.

Preparation and materials:

- Collect five different types of ads or circulars from a Sunday newspaper.

- Instruct students to make sure the ads are directed to somewhat different groups.

Procedure:

- Give each group of students a circular to examine. Selections might include a computer super store, a toy store, a food store, a car dealership, a home mainte-nance store, a drug store, or others that might be available.

  ▶ Divide the class into five groups.

  ▶ Each group will examine a circular.

  ▶ Each group will identify certain characteristics of the ad.

  ▶ Students will be able to determine the target audience

- Let the students look at and discuss the ads with each other.

  ▶ Ask these questions one by one:
    • To whom is this advertisement directed?
      • What factors determine this? (This will include such factors as age, gender, education level, financial success, and ethnic background.)
    • What styles of words or images are used?
    • Who created this message and why is the message being sent?
    • How did the ad attract your attention?
    • What point of view and values are represented in this message?
    • Is the content believable?
    • Will different people get different messages from this ad?
    • Who makes money from this?
    • What is left out of this message?

- Older students can examine the concept of stereotyping in ads for products designed for particular audiences.

Evaluation: Students will begin to understand that each message is clearly created for a specific reason, directed to a specific person, and scripted with that in mind.

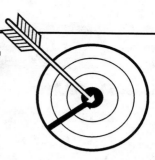

TARGET AUDIENCE ANALYSIS WORKSHEET

Directions: Circle or highlight the best answers and use the space on the right to write down the clues that helped you make your decision.

People in ad: What are they doing? What is their problem?	
Age of people in ad: Young child—elementary age or younger Middle-school and high-school age College age Young adult Older adult	
Gender: Male Female	
Do they look well educated? Yes No	
Do they look rich or poor? Rich Poor	
Can you tell where they are? At home In school In a car Traveling Somewhere else (be specific)	
Race: Black White Hispanic Asian Other	

Put all your facts together and describe the target audience:

_____

Activity 17   Changing the Target Audience

Grade levels: 4–8

Standards: Language Arts, Visual Arts

Activity description: Students will manipulate ads to change the target audience.

Preparation and materials:
- Divide class into small groups.

Procedure:
- Each group will be given a different circular to examine.
  - ► The groups will invent a new audience profile and change the wording or suggest a different image and answer these questions:
    - • What visual changes will appeal to the new audience?
    - • How can we maintain the audience's interest in our message?
    - • How can the new target audience understand the message best?
  - ► Students will share their new messages with the class.

Evaluation: Students will display knowledge of factors that determine a target audience.

Activity 18   Keeping an "Audience Journal"

Grade levels: 4–8

Standards: Language Arts, Visual Arts, Thinking and Reasoning

Activity description: Each student will record, for a week, a list of products he or she has seen advertised for that time period.

Preparation and materials:
- Students will create an "Audience Journal." This can be a section in a binder, a small notebook just for this journal, or a special folder. Have materials available for them. They may use copies of the Target Audience Analysis Worksheet (see page 15).

Procedure:
- As students see a product advertisement (message), they will record it into their Audience Journal. They will need to include the following information:
  - ► The product,
  - ► Where they encountered the message (TV, sign in a mall or store, newspaper, etc.),
  - ► The target audience of the message, and
  - ► Their reaction to the product message.

Evaluation: Students will begin to develop a broader awareness of media and their messages.

AUDIENCE JOURNAL

Name: _____

Product Advertised

Message Medium

Target Audience

Reaction

Date

Grade levels: 4–8

Standards: Visual Arts, Thinking and Reasoning

Activity description: Students will begin an examination of outdoor advertising.

Preparation and materials:
- Read the history of outdoor advertising.
- Have a whiteboard or chalkboard to scribe answers.

Procedure:
- Ask the students what kinds of outdoor advertising they have seen.
    - ▸ Answers might include:
        - Billboards
        - Bus signs
        - Bus shelters
        - Taxis
        - Airport signage
        - Stadium signs
        - Kiosks
        - Poster walls
        - Aerial banners and skywriting
- What message was the outdoor advertisement giving?
    - ▸ Scribe their answers.
- Where did they see the advertisement?
- Was the location of the advertisement related to the message?
- Was the message an advertisement for an item to purchase or for something else?
    - ▸ List the different intents.

Evaluation: Students will be able to understand that outdoor signage is another form of general advertising.

Related Internet Resources:
Outdoor Advertising Association of America (OAAA). *History of Outdoor.* 2002.
18 October 2003. <http://www.oaaa.org/outdoor/sales/history.asp>

Grade levels: 4–8

Standards: Visual Arts, Thinking and Reasoning

Activity description: Students will begin to examine and analyze billboard advertisements.

Preparation and materials:
- If you live in a location with billboards, photograph some of them for the class (students will be able to recognize them). If not, bookmark some Internet sites with billboard examples and have them ready for class examination. (See related Internet Resources.)

Procedure:
- Students will look at different billboard messages.
- Direct them to notice the differences in style as the culture changes.

Evaluation: Students will be able to recognize that the style of advertising changes as the popular culture changes.

Related Internet Resources:
Digital Scriptorium Rare Book, Manuscript and Special Collections Library of Duke University. *Historical Billboard Images.* 2000. Duke University. 17 October 2003. <http://scriptorium.lib.duke.edu/hartman/oa/billboard.html>

John W. Hartman Center for Sales, Advertising & Marketing History. Rare Book, Manuscript, and Special Collections Library. *The Outdoor Advertising Archives: An Introduction.* 2000. Duke University. 17 October 2003. <http://scriptorium.lib.duke.edu/hartman/oa/outdoor.html#define>

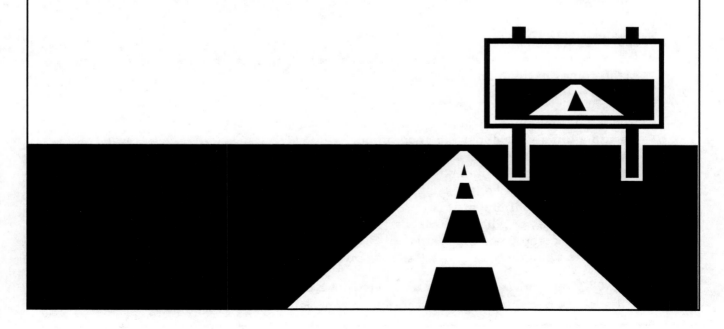

Activity 22 — Who Is the Billboard's Target Audience?

Grade levels: 4–8

Standards: Thinking and Reasoning, Working with Others, Language Arts, Visual Arts

Activity description: Students will be able to determine the target audience criteria for specific types of billboards.

Preparation and materials:
- From the discussion in the previous lesson, select several billboards that send different messages.
- Make copies of the billboards.
- Have a billboard target audience analysis sheet for each billboard.

Procedure:
- Divide students into groups.
- Assign a billboard to each group.
- Students will determine the target audience from the information they perceive from the billboard.
- Students will share their answers with the class.

Evaluation: Students will be able to determine the target audience of a billboard message.

Activity 23 — Reading the Billboard Message

Grade levels: 4–8

Standards: Behavioral Studies, Visual Arts, Thinking and Reasoning

Activity description: Students will be able to determine the message within the message in a billboard.

Preparation and materials:
- Have the target audience information available for students from previous activity.
- Make copies of the billboard message for each group.

Procedure:
- Divide students into the same group as the previous activity.
- Assign a different billboard to each group.
- Students will analyze the underlying message in the billboard.
- Students need to take into consideration:
    - Target audience
    - Location of billboard
    - Proximity of billboard to advertised place or event
    - Who created the billboard
    - The ultimate goal of the message on the billboard

Evaluation: Students will be able to deconstruct a billboard message and recognize that the location, target audience, and final intent determine the message.

Grade levels: 4–8

Standards: Visual Arts, Working with Others, Art Connections

Activity description: Students will create a class billboard.

Preparation and materials:
- Have materials available to create a billboard (large paper, poster boards, etc.).

Procedure:
- Brainstorm with the class to determine what message a billboard might be good for. Lead the class to at least the following possible answers. Be sure that students understand WHY for each of these.
    - Attention-getting by its big size
    - Cost-effective
        - A billboard can attract consumer attention without spending a fortune.
        - A billboard delivers the most audience for the least dollar spent.
        - A billboard requires little consumer effort to be seen.
        - A billboard is the only way to attract commuters on freeways and highways.
        - A good location can lead consumers right to your door.

Evaluation: Students will be able to determine when a billboard would be an appropriate medium.

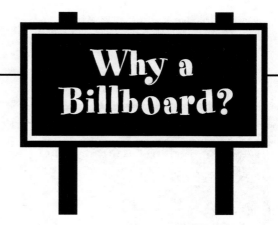

Grade levels: 4–8

Standards: Working with Others, Thinking and Reasoning

Activity description: The class will decide what it wants to do for a class billboard project.

Preparation and materials:
- Whiteboard or chalkboard to scribe student suggestions

Procedure:
- Consider the school building or campus as the "highway" for the billboard project. Students will have to decide the location where their message will have the most impact.

- Brainstorm with students to get ideas for a class billboard project. Since the billboard will be located in the school, it might have something to do with a regular school activity, an upcoming class election, or a special cause (endangered species, no smoking).
  - ▶ Be sure students consider location (in school), the message to be conveyed, and the elements of the target audience.

- Once a subject has been agreed upon, decide the different elements of construction that go into creating a billboard. Consider:
  - ▶ Construction,
  - ▶ Graphics, and
  - ▶ Message.

Evaluation: The class will agree with subject and design of billboard and will work together to create it.

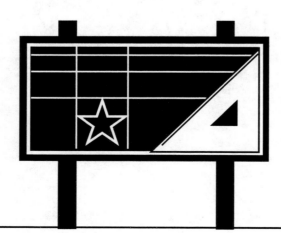

Grade levels: 4–8

Standards: Language Arts, Working with Others

Activity description: Students will evaluate common advertising slogans to determine if they are facts or opinions.

Preparation and materials:
- Whiteboard or chalkboard to record student answers

Procedure:
- Ask students to brainstorm and come up with some common or popular advertising slogans.

- Record the slogans on the whiteboard or chalkboard.

- One by one, discuss each slogan and try to determine if it is factual or based on an opinion that cannot be proven.

  ▶ "Bet you can't eat just one" (Lay's Potato Chips)

  ▶ Diamonds are forever (DeBeers)

  ▶ Just do it (Nike)

  ▶ The pause that refreshes (Coca-Cola)

  ▶ Tastes great, less filling (Miller Lite)

  ▶ We try harder (Avis)

  ▶ Good to the last drop (Maxwell House)

  ▶ Breakfast of champions (Wheaties)

  ▶ Does she ... or doesn't she? (Clairol)

  ▶ When it rains, it pours (Morton Salt)

  ▶ Where's the beef? (Wendy's)

Evaluation: Students will be able to determine if a slogan is based on opinion or is factual.

Related Internet Resources:
Braincandy. *Braincandy Word Play Collection: Advertising Slogans*. 1998–2002. Corsinet.com. 16 October 2003.
<http://www.corsinet.com/braincandy/slogans.html>

Media Analysis Worksheet

NAME _____

Directions: Answer the questions as best as you can by filling in the information as you see it.

Media being analyzed:

_____

Who (or what organization) has created this message and what is its purpose?

_____

Who is the target audience? Is the message designed especially for the audience?

_____

What lifestyles and values are being promoted?

_____

_____

What do you think the real message is?

_____

_____

Is there a viewpoint not presented?

_____

_____

Is the camera showing an honest view?

_____

Who owns this medium?

_____

Grade levels: 4–8

Standards: Visual Arts, Language Arts, Working with Others

Activity description: The students will think of additional marketing slogans they are familiar with and examine how they work.

Preparation and materials:

- Have the list of slogans from the previous lesson. These examples will help the students create their own slogans.

  ▶ Fun Trivia has an online slogan game. If you have access to the Internet, you might have the students complete this (see Related Internet Resources).

  ▶ Visit the University of Texas Web site for a wide variety of slogans that are or were famous.

Procedure:

- Students will look at famous slogans and talk about what makes them so catchy. By examining the phrasing, students will try to figure out the product (if they are not familiar with it) and the target audience.

Evaluation: The students will understand that certain phrases attract certain markets. They will understand about company image.

Related Internet Resources:

Fun Trivia:the Trivia Portal. *Identify the Business Sign*. 2002. 5 October 2002. <http://www.funtrivia.com/playquiz.cfm?qid=71214>

Richards, Jef I. The University of Texas at Austin Department of Advertising. *Texas Advertising*. 5 October 2002. <http://advertising.utexas.edu/world/>

AdAge.com. *Top 10 Slogans of the Century*. Crain Communicatons, Inc. 6 October 2002. <http://adage.com/century/slogans.html>

Activity 29   Create a Class Slogan

Grade levels: 4–8

Standard: Language Arts, Visual Arts, Working with Others

Activity description: Prior to creating their billboard, students will decide on their product slogan.

Preparation and materials:
- List of catchy common slogans
- Whiteboard or chalkboard to record brainstorming ideas

Procedure:
- The class will brainstorm to create a slogan for their billboard product or service.
- They will need to consider:
  - ▸ The images and values they want to promote,
  - ▸ The target audience, and
  - ▸ Whether the slogan will be factual or an opinion?

Evaluation: The class will create its slogan.

Activity 30   Creation of a Billboard: Implementation

Grade levels: 4–8

Standards: Visual Arts, Language Arts, Thinking and Reasoning

Activity description: The class will create a billboard.

Preparation and materials:
- Have materials on hand or available to assist students in completion of this project.

Procedure:
- Divide class into groups—each to handle a different element of the final product.
  - ▸ Construction
    - • The construction group will determine how the billboard should be constructed, e.g., posterboard, plywood, corrugated cardboard, paper, etc.
  - ▸ Graphics
    - • This group will do the actual design and painting of the billboard, but the entire class will decide the colors and images.
  - ▸ Message
    - • The message group will create the words to send the message. This group will need to remember to keep the concept simple so most people can understand it. The class will finalize the wording together.
- Remind the class that a simple message, strong design, and strategic placement are the components that help to fulfill your marketing objectives.

Evaluation: The class will complete the project and have the school community give feedback to determine its effectiveness.

Activity 31   Logo Recognition

Grade levels: 4–8

Standards: Visual Arts, Thinking and Reasoning

Activity description: Students will identify corporate logos.

Preparation and materials:
- Collect corporate logos from popular places.
  - ▶ McDonald's
  - ▶ Burger King
  - ▶ Nike
  - ▶ Coca Cola

Procedure:
- Show students the corporate logos.

- Ask students to identify each one.

- Ask what element makes recognition easy. Is it color? Is it the design?

- Why do corporations spend so much money advertising their corporate logos?

Evaluation: Students will identify factors that aid in logo recognition.

Activity 32   The Corporate Logo

Grade levels: 4–8

Standards: Visual Arts

Activity description: Students will look for corporate logos in the classroom.

Preparation and materials:
- Whiteboard or chalkboard to record logos

Procedure:
- Ask students to look at their clothing and identify any corporate logos. Have them include shoes, jackets, hats, etc.

- Ask students to look at their backpacks and all their other school supplies and find corporate logos.

Evaluation: Students will realize the large number of corporate logos that are easily seen.

Activity 33 — Logo Scavenger Hunt

Grade levels: 4–8

Standards: Visual Arts, Thinking and Reasoning

Activity description: Students will explore the school building and try to locate corporate logos in the building.

Preparation and materials:
- Clipboards; paper and pencils for students

Procedure:
- Take the class on a scavenger hunt through the school to see if students can locate any corporate logos in the building.
- Students will note where they see a corporate logo, identify which one it is, and try to guess why it's there on the Logo Investigation Chart.

Evaluation: Students will become aware that corporate logos/advertisements are everywhere, even in the school.

Activity 34 — Logo Mania

Grade levels: 4–8

Standard: Thinking and Reasoning, Visual Arts

Activity description: Students will discuss why logos are important to them.

Preparation and materials:
- Whiteboard or chalkboard to record answers

Procedure:
- Students can take 10 minutes to find as many logos as possible in the classroom.
- Record the most popular logos on the chalkboard or whiteboard.
- Ask students why these logos are so popular.
- Ask students if they can think of a reason why companies want their logos in as many public places as possible.

Evaluation: Students will understand that they actually can develop an allegiance to a product name.

Grade levels: 4–8

Standards: Mathematics, Thinking and Reasoning

Activity description: Students will learn about their group spending power.

Preparation and materials:

- Post these three questions on the whiteboard or chalkboard or on an overhead projector:

    1. Who spends about $300.00 each, per month, on non-essential items?

        a. single women   b. retired men   c. U.S. kids

    2. Which group spends a total of $11 to $15 billion each year?

        a. government lobbyists   b. foreign tourists   c. U.S. kids

    3. Which group influences the spending of about $160 billion of other peoples' money each year?

        a. celebrity spokespeople   b. N.Y. stockbrokers   c. U.S. kids

    The answer to each of those questions is, of course, c. U.S. kids.

Procedure:

- Discuss each choice with the class.

- Were students surprised by the answer?

- What does this mean to corporations and advertisers?

- How does this affect U.S. kids in their daily life?

Evaluation: Students will be aware of the spending power of their group.

Related Internet Resources:

Consumer's Union. *Captive Kids: A Report on Commercial Pressures on Kids at School.* 1998. 19 October 2003. <http://www.consumersunion.org/other/captivekids/problem.htm>

Starr, Linda. *From Billboard to Chalkboard: Advertising Creeps Into the Classroom.* 1998. Education World. 17 October 2003. <http://www.education-world.com/a_admin/admin056.shtml>

Activity 36   Bias: What Is a "Real Family"?

Grade levels: 4–8

Standards: Thinking and Reasoning

Activity description: Students will examine the variety in their own family units.

Preparation and materials:

■ Pictures from magazines and newspapers that portray a "family" (there are many possibilities)

■ Whiteboard or chalkboard to record student answers

Procedure:

■ Ask the students to define a family unit.

■ Have students share the make-up of their particular family units.

■ Students may use My Family Unit worksheet.

■ Chart similarities and differences:
   ▶ Is there a "typical" family in your class?
   ▶ What are the components?
   ▶ Do students think that this is the norm?

■ Ask students if they did this in another class in the building, would the results be the same?

■ Talk about the different types of families:
   ▶ Nuclear family with mother and father
   ▶ Single parent families
   ▶ Blended families: divorced parents; remarried parents; creating two homes for the children, each with a parent and a step-parent and possibly siblings and step-siblings
   ▶ Extended families: living with grandparents or other relatives
   ▶ Multiple-family household
   ▶ Foster parents
   ▶ Same sex parents

Evaluation: Students will understand that there are many different kinds of families.

Related Internet Resources:

Monash University. *The contemporary family: theoretical perspectives.* 2002. 16 October 2003. <http://www.arts.monash.edu.au/subjects/ssr/gsc1201/1.5/week7lec1/ sld002.htm>

Media Literacy. *Gender Equity.* Western Massachusetts Gender Equity Center. 16 October 2003. <http://www.genderequity.org/medialit/contents.html>

MY FAMILY UNIT WORKSHEET

NAME _____

Fill in the answers with information about your family.

FAMILY ROLES

		NAME OF PERSON
EMPLOYMENT: Works outside the home:	Works as:	
Works at home	Works as:	
Unemployed family member	Looking for a job?	
CLEANING: Cleans the house		
Does the laundry		
EATING: Type of food family eats	Fast Food Home cooking	
Each person eats on the run	Yes	No
Family eats together	Yes	No
Who cooks?		
Who cleans up after meals?		
Who shops for food?		
TRAVEL: How often? What kind of travel?		
DECISIONS: Who makes family decisions?		
RULES: Do you have family rules?		
Who enforces them?		
How?		
FUN: How does your family have fun?		

Grade levels: 4–8

Standards: Visual Arts, Working with Others, Language Arts

Activity description: Students will take a look at the media representation of the family unit and determine whether it is always accurate.

Preparation and materials:

- Have categories set up on the chalkboard or whiteboard for each type of family unit that is represented in your class (see previous activity).

- Have students keep a record of TV shows that they watch that portray a family unit.

Procedure:

- Students will bring in their list of TV shows that portray a family unit.

- Have students place the name of the program in the family category that best fits it.

  ▶ Do all shows have a place or are they different than the ones represented in the class?

  ▶ Create new categories for the ones that don't fit, but use a different color marker.

  ▶ Ask students if they think these TV representations are just ones that don't fit with those of the class or are they constructed?

Evaluation: Students will understand that the representations made by the media are not always accurate and recognize that the media constructs its own reality.

Related Internet Resources:

For a great explanation on why the media uses stereotypes see:
Media Awareness Network. *Once Upon a Time*. 1997. 16 October 2003.
<http://www.media-awareness.ca/eng/med/class/teamedia/onceupon.htm>

Grade levels: 4–8

Standards: Visual Arts, Language Arts, Working with Others

Activity description: Students will examine TV families and look for stereotypes.

Preparation and materials:
- Record excerpts from several TV shows that portray a family unit.
  - ► Use drama, sitcoms, or even the popular cartoon families.
  - ► Be sure to include some of the ones the students watch regularly.

Procedure:
- Students will watch TV clips.

- Students will discuss:
  - ► How are these family representations different than the ones in the class?
  - ► Why are they constructed this way?
  - ► Whether stereotypes help you understand stories better?

Evaluation: Students will understand the family stereotypes that are represented in the media.

MY LIFE VS. TV LIFE

Name: _____ **Name of TV character:** _____

After watching several TV shows, think about comparing your life to the life of a child on television. Fill in the table as honestly as possible.

My real life	TV character Life
My afterschool life	TV character afterschool life
My friends	TV character friends
My house	TV character house
My family life	TV character family life
My real Mom	TV character Mom
My real Dad	TV character Dad

Gender Bias: What Makes Up a Real Girl?
What Makes Up a Real Boy?

Grade levels: 4–8

Standards: Thinking and Reasoning, Language Arts

Activity description: Students will explore different representations of their genders.

Preparation and materials:

- A gender worksheet for each student

Procedure:

- Have each student complete a gender worksheet. Ask students to be honest about their answers, even if they feel they are unusual.

- Divide the chalkboard or whiteboard into two columns: one Male (Boy) and one Female (Girl).

- Record adjectives students wrote for themselves.

Evaluation: Students will become aware of how they describe themselves in relation to gender.

GENDER WORKSHEET

Name:_____

Directions: Fill in the worksheet categories as honestly as you can.

1. My gender is:

    Male   Female

2. Five adjectives I'd use to describe my physical self are:

    _____

    _____

    _____

    _____

    _____

3. My favorite things to do after school are:

    _____

    _____

    _____

    _____

    _____

4. What does it mean to "act like a boy"?

5. What does it mean to "act like a girl"?

6. How do you and your behavior differ from the stereotype?

Activity 43   Gender Bias: What's Wrong with This Picture?

Grade levels: 4–8

Standards: Visual Arts, Thinking and Reasoning, Language Arts

Activity description: Students will begin their exploration of gender representation and bias in print materials.

Preparation and materials:
- Collect pictures from age-appropriate magazines that picture boys or girls in an activity.
- Collect advertisements from sources that depict boys and girls in play.
- Collect advertisements for toys and products specifically marketed to boys or girls.
- Display these materials in the classroom.

Procedure:
- Students will look at the photographs.
- They will vote whether they think the representation of boys or girls is fair and correct.

Evaluation: Students will be able to determine the target audience of an advertisement and determine whether it is realistic or not.

Activity 44   Gender Bias: Is That the Toy for Me?

Grade levels: 4–8

Standards: Language Arts, Visual Arts

Activity description: Students will examine specific toy advertisements in print and determine the truth in advertising.

Preparation and materials:
- Use advertisements from the previous activity.
- Collect toy advertisements in print that specifically target boys or girls.

Procedure:
- Let students look at all the ads.
- Students will group ads into two categories: boys and girls.
- Talk about how the ad represents the toy, if it is realistic, and does the fact that it targets a boy or a girl make a child of the other gender hesitate to use it?
    - Do boys ever play with dolls?
    - Do girls ever play with guns?
    - Why aren't boys and girls represented truly in the advertisements?
- Are the children in the ads realistically represented?
    - Do they look like real kids?
    - Are they the right age for the toy?
    - Are these children made to look perfect?

Evaluation: Students will begin to evaluate advertisements for fairness and honesty.

Activity 45   Are You the Target Audience?

Grade levels: 4–8

Standards: Thinking and Reasoning, Language Arts, Visual Arts

Activity description: Students will examine toy advertisements in print and determine the target audience.

Preparation and materials:
- Use the toy advertisements from the previous activity.

Procedure:
- Divide the class into small groups.
- Give each group a toy advertisement.
- Each group will determine the target audience and the purpose of the advertisement.

Evaluation: Students will understand the target audience of toy ads.

Activity 46   Will Changing the Audience Alter the Appeal of the Toy?

Grade levels: 4–8

Standard: Thinking and Reasoning, Language Arts, Visual Arts

Activity description: Groups from previous activity will rewrite the ad, and by changing the target audience, they will also change the effectiveness of the ad.

Preparation and materials:
- Use the toy advertisements from the previous activity and the target audience analysis papers.

Procedure:
- Each group will have the opportunity to change the target audience for the ad.
- The groups will rewrite the ad to fit their new target audience.
- They will present their new ads to the class and discuss the following:
  ▶ Does the toy have the same appeal to a different audience?
  ▶ By changing the audience, does the market effect also change?
  ▶ Is the new audience likely to buy the toy?
  ▶ Who decides who should buy the toy?

Evaluation: Students will begin to understand the power of wording in the media.

Activity 47 — Toys on TV

Grade levels: 4–8

Standards: Thinking and Reasoning, Language Arts

Activity description: Students will compare toy ads that appear in print with toy ads on TV.

Preparation and materials:
- Record toy ads for popular toys from TV.
- Find the same toy in a print ad and present it to the class.

Procedure:
- The class will watch the series of toy ads that you have recorded.
- Students will examine the print ads that present the same toy.
- Divide the class into groups and have them evaluate and compare both ads.
- Discuss the results.

Evaluation: Students will be able to evaluate the validity of toy ads and point out differences in types of advertising for the same types of items.

Activity 48 — TV Toys

Grade levels: 4–8

Standards: Higher Level Thinking, Visual Arts, Language Arts

Activity description: Students will investigate toys that are advertised on TV.

Preparation and materials:
- Record toy ads from TV.

Procedure:
- Students will watch the toy ads.
- With the class, discuss the pros and cons of TV toy ads.
- Questions to inspire discussion might be:
  - Does the ad exaggerate the toy's performance?
  - Does the toy require special skills and abilities that aren't mentioned?
  - Are all the pieces included in the sale package? (e.g., batteries)
  - Is the setting in which the toy is shown realistic or imaginary?
  - Does the toy need assembly? Does the ad mention that?
  - Is the toy age-appropriate for the child who will want it?
  - Is the toy merchandised for a TV program?

Evaluation: Students will understand that advertisements may sometimes be misleading.

Related Internet Resources:
The Brookline Area Community Council Web. *Toy Ads On TV—Facts For Consumers.*
17 October 2003. <http://trfn.clpgh.org/bacc/Safety/Toys.html>

Grade levels: 4–8

Standards: Higher Level Thinking, Visual Arts, Language Arts

Activity description: Students will examine the connection of toy advertisements with TV shows, food chains, movies, and other media events.

Preparation and materials:
- Bring in the following for toys linked with a TV show, food chain, or movie:
  - ▶ Print ads
  - ▶ TV ads
  - ▶ The actual toys (if you have access to them)

- Whiteboard or chalkboard to record student answers

Procedure:
- Toys are often advertised with a fast food purchase.
  - ▶ Ask students to list some of the ones they remember.
    - • How might this influence selection of a meal?

- Toys are sometimes linked with cartoon characters or regular TV shows.
  - ▶ Ask students to list some of the ones they remember.
    - • Which came first: the cartoon, the show, or the toy?
  - ▶ Do they think that the toy makes the TV show more popular?

- Toys are often linked with movie productions.
  - ▶ Ask students to list some of the ones they remember.
    - • Did the toy enhance your enjoyment of the movie?
    - • Did you see the movie first or buy the toy first?
    - • Was the toy satisfactory to you?
    - • Do you think that the toy was manufactured for children to play with or to promote the movie?

Evaluation: Students will begin to see the connection between advertising a toy product and the sale of another product.

Related Internet Resources:
Young Media Australia. *Toy Advertising.* 2002. 17 October 2003.
<http://www.youngmedia.org.au/mediachildren/03_06_ads_toys.htm>

Grade levels: 4–8

Standards: Thinking and Reasoning, Language Arts, Visual Arts

Activity description: Students will express their opinions on the honesty of toy advertisements.

Preparation and materials:
- Sunday circular from a toy store

- Christmas catalogs from toy stores and large department stores (e.g., J.C. Penney's Dream Book)

Procedure:
- Ask students if they have ever purchased a toy after viewing an ad in the paper or in a catalog.

- Have them look for the toys in your selection of advertisements.

- Ask them:
    ▶ Was the toy represented honestly?
    ▶ Could it do all the things the ad mentioned?
    ▶ Did it affect your life the way the ad might have suggested?
    ▶ Did you want to buy it before you saw the ad, or did the ad persuade you to ask your parents to purchase it?
    ▶ Were you happy with the toy?
    ▶ Did it last?
    ▶ Was the advertised price a fair one?
    ▶ Was the toy available when your parents went to the store or was it out of stock?

Evaluation: Using personal experience as a basis, students will be able to evaluate the validity of a printed toy ad.

Activity 51   Buy My Toy I

Grade levels: 2, 3, 4, and 5

Standard: Language Arts

Activity description: Students will create a print advertisement for their favorite toys.

Preparation and materials:
- Ask students to bring in their favorite toys.

Procedure:
- Class members will display their favorite toys.
- Students will design a print advertisement for their toys.

Evaluation: Students will incorporate all the elements of a good advertisement.

Activity 52   Buy My Toy II

Grade levels: 2, 3, 4, and 5

Standards: Language Arts, Visual Arts, Working with Others

Activity description: Students will peer edit each other's ads.

Preparation and materials:
- Ask students to bring their favorite toys to class.

Procedure:
- Students will peer edit each other's ads, using a criteria list for good advertisements.
- Students will present their completed ads to the class.

Evaluation: Students will incorporate all the elements of a good advertisement.

Activity 53   Create a Commercial for Your Favorite Toy

Grade levels: 4–8

Standards: Visual Arts, Language Arts

Activity description: Using their favorite toys and the information from their print advertisement, students will create and record a commercial advertisement.

Preparation and materials:
- Video camera

Procedure:
- Students will write a script for a 30-second TV commercial to sell their favorite toys.
- Students will have to incorporate speech and facial expressions.
- Commercials will be videotaped.
- Students will watch each commercial segment and evaluate the results.

Evaluation: Each student will create a 30-second taped commercial for their favorite toys, incorporating all the elements of a good advertisement.

Activity 54   Photography: The Skill Behind the Image

Grade levels: 4–8

Standard: Visual Arts

Activity description: Students will talk about the concept of photographs and the specific responses they are designed to elicit.

Preparation and materials:
- Collect a series of photographs (they can be advertisements) that might evoke specific emotional responses from the students. (The American Memory Collection is a good source at <http://memory.loc.gov/>.)
- Display these photos around the room.

Procedure:
- Divide students into groups.
- Each group of students will:
  - ▶ Examine a group of photos.
  - ▶ Write as many words as they can to describe the photos.
  - ▶ Decide which techniques the photographer used to enhance the photo's impact:
    - Angle,
    - Focus,
    - Lighting,
    - Background, and
    - Coloring.
- Students will share their feelings.

Evaluation: Students will be able to connect certain artistic elements used in photography to emotional responses in viewers.

Grade levels: 4–8

Standards: Visual Arts, Thinking and Reasoning

Activity description: Students will examine photos from advertisements and decide what each ad is really trying to sell.

Preparation and materials:
- Select photographic advertisements that might not clearly represent what each ad is for.
- Cover the text in the photo ads and display them around the room.

Procedure:
- Students will examine the ads and record what they think each ad is trying to sell
- Students will share their opinions and observations.
- After the class discussion, show them the full ads and discuss them further:
  - ▶ Are students surprised? Why?
  - ▶ How did the photographer fool them? Why might this have been done?

Evaluation: Students will be able to recognize how an ad might really misrepresent a product.

Grade levels: 4–8

Standards: Visual Arts, Thinking and Reasoning

Activity description: Students will examine the photographs of the children in the toy ads.

Preparation and materials:
- Whiteboard or chalkboard
- Overhead projector
- Look through magazines and pick several advertisements that are aimed at the age level of the students in your class. You will need to find some that have both male and female images. Copy the ads to an overhead transparency.

Procedure:
- The students will carefully look at one of the pictures.
- Ask them to describe what they see.
  ▶ Write the comments on a whiteboard or chalkboard.
- Lead them in the discussion to be sure they comment on everything that is in the picture.
- After they complete the description of the picture, ask them to explain what the picture means.
  ▶ Write down the comments on a whiteboard of chalkboard.
  ▶ Compare the answers, as the picture might mean something different to different students.

Evaluation: Students will understand that different people might get a different message from the same photo.

Grade levels: 4–8

Standards: Visual Arts, Thinking and Reasoning

Activity description: Students will examine the ads used in the previous activity and start talking about the techniques used to enhance photographs.

Preparation and materials:

- Put the photograph that was described and analyzed in the previous activity on the overhead projector.

Procedure:

- Begin asking students to look for various aspects of the photograph (even very young children can do this):
    - ► How has color been used?
    - ► What angle of camera shots has been used?
    - ► What is cropped out of the picture? (cut out)
    - ► Is the photograph a close-up or a distance photograph?
    - ► Is everything in the background clear?
    - ► Is the setting realistic?

- Do all these elements affect the students' desire to buy the advertised product?

- Why?

Evaluation: Students will begin to understand that photographs are designed to appeal to a certain audience and to make the viewer want to purchase the product.

Grade levels: 4–8

Standards: Visual Arts, Thinking and Reasoning

Activity description: Students will have an opportunity to examine a camera.

Preparation and materials: (These will depend on what is available.)

■ A digital camera, if your school has one—this is the best choice

■ A regular 35 millimeter camera

■ A throwaway camera

Procedure:

■ Students will look at a chart that describes the parts of a camera and talk about how each part works and what it does.

■ If there is more than one type available, discussion can follow dealing with the differences among them.
   ▶ Speed of delivery (picture)
   ▶ Type of uses

Evaluation: Students will understand that there are different kinds of still cameras.

Related Internet Resources:

There are many excellent sites that can prepare you for teaching the basic parts and their function in a camera.

NEC Electron Devices. *Digital Still Camera Diagram*. 1995–2002. 14 October 2003. <http://www.ic.nec.co.jp/micro/english/application/digicame/digcame.html>

Houston, Alistair. *The SLR Camera*. Silverlight Co. 2000. 14 October 2003. <http://www.silverlight.co.uk/tutorials/camera/camera_diagram.html>

Grade levels: 4–8

Standards: Visual Arts, Thinking and Reasoning

Activity description: Students will examine photographs of themselves and discuss the variables that make one picture better or more flattering than another.

Preparation and materials:
- Students will be assigned to collect and bring in a small collection of photos of themselves, representing different times in their lives.

Procedure:
- Students will display their photos.
  - ► Each photo will have a number assigned to it.
- There will be a checklist for each photo.
- Students will go around the room and evaluate each set of photos according to the criteria on the checklist.
- Students will talk about their findings.

Evaluation: Students will be able to identify a good photo and explain what makes it better than another.

Photo Checklist

Name: _____

1. View the photo, then close your eyes.
   What image stands out in your mind?

   _____

2. What idea is being expressed?

   _____

3. How does this picture make you feel?

   _____

4. Does it have good use of color?

   _____

5. What is the angle of the camera shot?

   _____

6. What caption would you write for this photo?

   _____

7. What is cropped out or cut-out of the picture?

   _____

8. Is the photograph a close-up or a distance photograph?

   _____

9. Is everything in the background clear?

   _____

10. Is the setting realistic?

    _____

Activity 61 — Photographs: Lighting

Grade levels: 4–8

Standards: Visual Arts, Thinking and Reasoning

Activity description: The importance of good lighting in a photograph will be examined.

Preparation and materials:
- Read the Kodak tutorial on lighting at this Kodak site and select "lighting."
  - ► <http://www.kodak.com/eknec/PageQuerier.jhtml?pq-path=38/315&pq-locale=en_US>
- If a computer lab is available, take the students to the lab and have them explore this site together.
- If there is no lab available, prepare overhead transparencies with this information.

Procedure:
- Students will explore how using and changing light can alter a photograph.

Evaluation: The class will be able to identify the type of light used in a photo.

Related Internet Resources:
Eastman Kodak. *The Language of Light Classroom.* 1994–2002. 13 October 2002.
<http://www.kodak.com/eknec/PageQuerier.jhtml?pq-path=38/315/338&pq-locale=en_US>

Activity 62 — Photographs: Composition

Grade levels: 4–8

Standards: Visual Arts, Thinking and Reasoning

Activity description: The students will explore the basics of good photographic composition.

Preparation and materials:
- Read the Kodak tutorial on composition at this Kodak site. Select "composing your pictures."
  - ► <http://www.kodak.com/eknec/PageQuerier.jhtml?pq-path=38/315/332&pq-locale=en_US>
- If a computer lab is available, take the students to the lab and have them explore this site together.
- If there is no lab available, prepare overhead transparencies with this information.

Procedure:
- Students will explore the components of photographic composition.
- Be sure to encourage discussion about this topic among students.

Evaluation: The class will develop an understanding of photographic composition.

Related Internet Resources:
Eastman Kodak. *Composition: Guide to Better Pictures.* 1994–2002. 18 October 2003.
<http://www.kodak.com/eknec/PageQuerier.jhtml?pq-path=332&pq-locale=en_US>

Grade levels: 4–8

Standards: Visual Arts, Thinking and Reasoning

Activity description: Students will explore the rule of thirds, one of the basic components of good photography composition.

Preparation and materials:

- Read the Kodak information on Rule of Thirds at this Kodak site (see page 7).

    ► <http://www.kodak.com/global/en/consumer/education/lessonPlans/guides/picTake.pdf>

- If a computer lab is available, take the students to the lab and have them explore this site together.

- If there is no lab available, prepare overhead transparencies with this information.

Procedure:

- Students will look at the most basic component of a good photograph, the center of interest, in this Rule of Thirds tutorial.

Evaluation: Students will now have a basic understanding of the elements of a good photograph.

Related Internet Resources:

Eastman Kodak. *Composition: Guide to Better Pictures.* 1994–2002. 18 October 2003. <http://www.kodak.com/global/en/consumer/education/lessonPlans/guides/picTake.pdf>

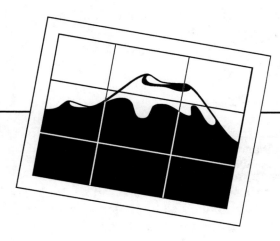

Activity 64 | Digital Imaging: The Fantasy I

These lessons are for schools with access to a digital camera and the Internet.

Grade levels: 4–8

Standards: Visual Arts, Thinking and Reasoning, Art Connections

Activity description: Students will select a celebrity they admire, locate a photograph of the celebrity, then copy and save it.

Preparation and materials:
■ Internet access

Procedure:
■ Have each student pick a celebrity (athlete, performer, musician, etc.) that he or she admires or would like to be. Make sure students select celebrities of their same gender.

■ Have students search the Internet for a photograph of their celebrity.

■ Students will copy and save the picture, also citing the bibliographic information for the picture.

Evaluation: Students will be able to locate a photograph of an admired personality and cite the source.

Activity 65 | Digital Imaging: The Fantasy II

Grade levels: 4–8

Standards: Visual Arts, Thinking and Reasoning, Art Connections

Activity description: Students will learn to use a digital camera, take pictures of each other, upload the files, and save them.

Preparation and materials:
■ Digital camera

Procedure:
■ Each student will evaluate the angle of the celebrity's face in the picture they selected in the previous lesson.

■ This part of the lesson requires close teacher supervision.
  ► Students will photograph each other, trying to duplicate the angle of the celebrity's face. This will need to be a close-up.
  ► Pictures will be uploaded, named, and saved.

Evaluation: Students will be able to use a digital camera to take a simple photograph and analyze an existing photo.

Grade levels: 4–8

Standards: Visual Arts, Thinking and Reasoning, Art Connections

Activity description: Students will create a new celebrity by cutting their faces and pasting them onto the celebrity's picture.

Preparation and materials:
- Become familiar with your digital imaging software.
  - ▶ You might want to practice this several times so you can demonstrate it better to the students.

Procedure:
- In the computer lab, each student will open up the digital imaging software.

- Each student will open the picture of the celebrity and the picture of themselves.

- Students will manipulate their photos.
  - ▶ With the lasso tool, crop their face, neck and hair in a way that best fits the celebrity photo.
  - ▶ Let students repeat this until they are satisfied with the results.

- Students will manipulate the celebrity photo.
  - ▶ Copy the selection from the photo file.
  - ▶ With the celebrity photo open, choose Edit > Paste > As New Layer.
  - ▶ Students will move the selection until it is in the best position possible.
  - ▶ Students will use tools to blend the places where the images meet.

- When students are satisfied with their images, they will save them with new names.

- Have students share their new "celebrities" with each other and talk about how this process can manipulate the truth.

- Possible discussion: Can we believe what we see?

- Print out their new photos for a class bulletin board.

Evaluation: Students will create a new image with their faces on the body of a celebrity using digital imaging software.

Grade levels: 4–8

Standards: Visual Arts, Thinking and Reasoning, Art Connections

Activity description: Class will visit the PBS Web site and see how the photo on the cover of a magazine is prepared.

Preparation and materials:
- Internet access for class or an LCD projector with one computer hooked up to this Web site
  - ▶ PBS Don't Buy It: Get Media Smart. Secrets of a Cover Model Revealed <http://pbskids.org/dontbuyit/ entertainment/covermodel_1.html>

Procedure:
- The class will view or navigate to the PBS Web site.

- Together, go over the five pages in this presentation and talk about each one.

- Discuss and record:
  - ▶ The model's comments,
  - ▶ The number of products used to prepare her for the shoot, and
  - ▶ The number of people it takes to prepare her for the shoot.

- Be sure to explore the BEFORE and AFTER shots on the Computer Touch-Up page.
  - ▶ Ask students how they feel about the changes made to her body with computer touchups.

- Invite the students to talk about how this makes them feel.

Evaluation: Students will learn more tricks of creating a photo for the media.

Related Internet Resources:
PBS Kids. *Don't Buy It: Get Media Smart. Secrets of a Cover Model Revealed.* 2002. 16 October 2003. <http://pbskids.org/dontbuyit/entertainment/ covermodel_1.html>

Grade levels: 4–8

Standards: Visual Arts, Thinking and Reasoning, Language Arts

Activity description: Students will examine and evaluate food advertisements.

Preparation and materials:
■ Collect food advertisements from various media. Be sure to include a variety of ads such as fast foods, cereals, desserts, candy, and a health food product.

Procedure:
■ Divide the class into groups. Each group will be given a picture of a food to examine.

■ Each group will deconstruct the ad to determine:

　　► Who is the target audience?

　　► What is being advertised?

　　► Who created the advertisement?

　　► Whether the picture is realistic?

　　► Whether the ad motivates the student to buy the product?

Evaluation: Students will be able to critically evaluate a food ad.

Grade levels: 4–8

Standards: Visual Arts, Thinking and Reasoning, Language Arts

Activity description: Students will examine the packaging of some food products.

Preparation and materials:

■ Collect and display a variety of food products.

■ Use products that might have unusual spellings for words, such as "froot" instead of fruit.

Procedure:

■ Divide students into groups.

■ Each group will examine a food package and analyze its construction:
  ▶ Size of box
  ▶ Type of lettering on the package
  ▶ Number of places lettering appears
  ▶ Color of the box
  ▶ Picture on front of box
  ▶ Location of important information on box

■ Students should also answer the following questions:
  ▶ What age group does the food appeal to (and why does it appeal to that age group)?
  ▶ How does this company sell their product to the target audience?
  ▶ What is the approximate price of the product?
  ▶ Where are the list of ingredients and the nutritional values located on the box?

■ Students will discuss their findings.

Evaluation: Students will be able to deconstruct a food package.

Related Internet Resources:

For some great ideas and input: PBS Kids.
Don't Buy It: Get Media Smart. 2002. 16 October 2003.
<http://pbskids.org/dontbuyit/teachersguide.htm.>

Activity 70   Don't Buy It

Grade levels: 4–8

Standards: Visual Arts, Thinking and Reasoning, Language Arts

Activity description: Students will take an Internet journey to the PBS Web site, "Don't Buy It: Get Media Smart."

Preparation and materials:
- Internet access

Procedure:
- If there are enough computers available, each student will log onto the site. If there are not enough computers, set up teams for student work.
- Go to the PBS Kids Web site at http://pbskids.org/dontbuyit/advertisingtricks/foodadtricks.html>.
- Let students browse the "Food Advertising Tricks" section.
- Discuss the fact that what you see in an ad has nothing to do with real food.

Evaluation: Students will be aware that the food shown in ads is as doctored up, as is a model on a front cover of a magazine.

Related Internet Resources:
PBS Kids. *Food Advertising Tricks You Should Know About.* 2002. 18 October 2003. <http://pbskids.org/dontbuyit/advertisingtricks/foodadtricks.html>

Activity 71   PBS Web Site

Grade levels: 4–8

Standards: Visual Arts, Thinking and Reasoning, Language Arts

Activity description: Students will explore the "Advertising Tricks" section of the PBS Kids Web site.

Preparation and materials:
- Internet access

Procedure:
- If there are enough computers available, each student will log onto the site. If there are not enough computers, set up teams for student work.
- Go to the PBS Kids Web site at http://pbskids.org/dontbuyit/advertisingtricks/>.
- Let students browse the rest of the "Food Advertising Tricks" section, including the "Create Your Own Ads" section and "Create Your Own Cereal Box."
- Students will share their ads.

Evaluation: Students will be able to demonstrate an understanding of the creation of an advertisement.

Related Internet Resources:
PBS Kids. *Don't Buy It. Advertising Tricks. Discover the Secrets of Selling.* 2002. 17 October 2003. <http://pbskids.org/dontbuyit/advertisingtricks/>

Grade levels: 4–8

Standards: Thinking and Reasoning, Language Arts

Activity description: Students will look at the few big media industry shareholders and what they own.

Preparation and materials:

- Read and explore the sites in the Internet Resources for this activity.

- Prepare charts for the class that will be easy for students to understand, with corporations that they have probably heard of.

Procedure:

- Write these corporate names on the board. See if students recognize any of them.
  - ► AOL/Time Warner
  - ► Disney/ABC/CAP
  - ► Bertelsmann
  - ► Viacom/Paramount
  - ► News Corporation/FOX Network
  - ► SONY
  - ► General Electric/NBC
  - ► Westinghouse/CBS

- Reveal what is owned by each corporation.
  - ► **AOL/Time Warner**
    - America Online (AOL) acquired Time Warner—the largest merger in corporate history.
    - CNN, HBO, Cinemax, TBS Superstation, Turner Network Television, Turner Classic Movies, Warner Brothers Television, Cartoon Network, Sega Channel, TNT, Comedy Central (50%), E! (49%), Court TV (50%).
    - Largest owner of cable systems in the United States with an estimated 13 million subscribers.
    - HBO Independent Productions, Warner Home Video, New Line Cinema, Castle Rock, Looney Tunes, Hanna-Barbera.
    - Music: Atlantic, Elektra, Rhino, Sire, Warner Bros. Records, EMI, WEA, Sub Pop (distribution) = the world's largest music company.
    - 33 magazines including *Time*, *Sports Illustrated*, *People*, *In Style*, *Fortune*, *Book of the Month Club*, *Entertainment Weekly*, *Life*, *DC Comics* (50%), and *MAD Magazine*.
    - Sports: The Atlanta Braves, The Atlanta Hawks, World Championship Wrestling.
  - ► **Disney/ABC/CAP**
    - ABC: includes 10 stations, 24% of US households.
    - ABC Network News: *Prime Time Live*, *Nightline*, *20/20*, *Good Morning America*.
    - ESPN, Lifetime Television (50%), as well as minority holdings in A&E, History Channel, and E!
    - Disney Channel/Disney Television, Touchstone Television.
    - Miramax, Touchstone Pictures.

- Magazines: *Jane, Los Angeles Magazine, W, Discover*.
- Three music labels, 11 major local newspapers.
- Hyperion book publishers.
- Infoseek Internet search engine (43%).
- Sid R. Bass (major shares) crude oil and gas.
- All Disney Theme Parks, Walt Disney Cruise Lines.

► **Bertelsmann**
- The Ballantine Publishing Group, Bantam Dell Publishing Group, Crown Publishing Group, Doubleday Broadway Publishing Group, Knopf Publishing Group, Random House Publishing Group.
- Barnesandnoble.com.
- Magazines include: *American Homestyle, Child, Family Circle, Fitness, Inc., Jump, Parents, YM Magazine*.
- Online companies: bs medic, Sport 1, Lycos Europe, CD Now, MyMusic.com, Napster (partial investment), MusicNet.
- BMG Music Group: Arista Records, RCA, RCA Victor, BMG Classics, BMG Music Publishing, BMG Music Service, BMG Special Products, Windham Hill Group.

► **Viacom**
- Paramount Television, Spelling Television, MTV, VH-1, Showtime, The Movie Channel, UPN (joint owner), Nickelodeon, Comedy Central, Sundance Channel (joint owner), Flix.
- 20 major market U.S. stations.
- Paramount Pictures, Paramount Home Video, Blockbuster Video, Famous Players Theatres, Paramount Parks.
- Simon & Schuster Publishing.

► **News Corporation/FOX Network (Rupert Murdoch)**
- Fox Television: includes 22 stations, 50% of U.S. households.
- Fox International: extensive worldwide cable and satellite networks include British Sky Broadcasting (40%); VOX, Germany (49.9%); Canal Fox, Latin America; FOXTEL, Australia (50%); STAR TV, Asia; IskyB, India; Bahasa Programming Ltd., Indonesia (50%); and News Broadcasting, Japan (80%).
- The Golf Channel (33%).
- Twentieth Century Fox, Fox Searchlight.
- 132 newspapers (113 in Australia alone) including the *New York Post*, the *London Times*, and *The Australian*.
- 25 magazines including *TV Guide* and *The Weekly Standard*.
- HarperCollins books.
- Sports: LA Dodgers, LA Kings, LA Lakers, National Rugby League.
- Ansett Australia airlines, Ansett New Zealand airlines.
- Rupert Murdoch: Board of Directors, Philip Morris (USA).

► **SONY**
- Sony Corporation of America.
- Sony Music Entertainment, Inc.
- Columbia Records Group, Epic Records Group, Harmony Records, Legacy Recordings, Loud Records, Monument, Lucky Dog, Sony Music Soundtrax, and Sony Wonder (children's/family unit).

- Sony Picture Entertainment: Columbia TriStar Motion Picture Group, Screen Gems, Sony Pictures Television Group.
- Sony Electronics, Inc.
- Sony Computer Entertainment America, Inc.
- Metreon—A Sony Entertainment Center.
- Sony Plaza Public Arcade & Sony Wonder Technology Lab.

▶ **General Electric/NBC**
- NBC: includes 13 stations, 28% of U.S. households.
- NBC Network News: *The Today Show*, *Nightly News with Tom Brokaw*, *Meet the Press*, *Dateline NBC*, *NBC News at Sunrise*.
- CNBC business television; MSNBC 24-hour cable and Internet news service (co-owned by NBC and Microsoft); Court TV (co-owned with Time Warner); Bravo (50%); A&E (25%); History Channel (25%).
- GE Consumer Electronics.
- GE Power Systems: produces turbines for nuclear reactors and power plants.
- GE Plastics: produces military hardware and nuclear power equipment.
- GE Transportation Systems: runs diesel and electric trains.

▶ **Westinghouse/CBS**
- CBS: includes 14 stations and over 200 affiliates in the United States.
- CBS Network News: *60 minutes*, *48 hours*, *CBS Evening News with Dan Rather*, *CBS Morning News*, *Up to the Minute*.
- Country Music Television, The Nashville Network, two regional sports networks.
- Group W Satellite Communications.
- Westinghouse Electric Company: provides services to the nuclear power industry.
- Westinghouse Government Environmental Services Company: disposes of nuclear and hazardous wastes. Also operates four government-owned nuclear power plants in the United States.
- Energy Systems: provides nuclear power plant design and maintenance.

Evaluation: Students will become aware that only a few companies are in control of most of the media messages we get.

Related Internet Resources:

Adbusters. *Media Carta. Who owns what?* 16 October 2003. <http://www.adbusters.org/campaigns/mediacarta/toolbox/who_owns/>

Chamisa Mesa High School. *Corporations: Understanding Their Media is Understanding Their Mission.* 16 October 2003. <http://www.chamisamesa.net/corp.html>

Moore, Aaron. *Who Owns What?* Columbia Journalism Review. 16 October 2003. <http://www.cjr.org/owners/bertelsmann.asp>

Grade levels: 4–8

Standards: Thinking and Reasoning, Language Arts

Activity description: With the knowledge that only a few corporations control the media, students will brainstorm to determine how their messages might be biased.

Preparation and materials:
- Have the chart of the Disney Corporation ready for students to look at.

Procedure:
- Ask students to think about what Disney means to them.
- Record all answers. There are no wrong answers.
- Bring the chart that lists the corporations that Disney owns.
- Cross-reference the corporations to the meaning the students have of Disney.
- Ask students to think about why Disney owns so many companies and why its name is on so many products.
- Do they think that Disney messages may be biased? Why? Why not?

Evaluation: Students will be able to understand the implications of a corporation sending media messages.

Grade levels: 4–8

Standards: Visual Arts, Thinking and Reasoning, Language Arts

Activity description: Students will examine some of the mass quantity of junk mail that is sent to their homes.

Preparation and materials:

■ One month prior to this activity, draft a letter to the parents of your students requesting that they save the junk mail that arrives at their homes for a month. Depending on the age/grade of your students, ask parents to help their children sort the mail into several groups:

- ► Envelopes with the words "urgent," "immediate," or "open at once" on the front
- ► Words that say there is something free inside
- ► An envelope with no return address
- ► A window envelope with a "check" (or so it seems) inside, or a statement on the envelope that a check is enclosed
- ► A sales pitch inviting you to join something with "no obligation"
- ► A post card stating that you have won something and need to claim it by calling "this number"
- ► Envelopes made to look like they were sent via express mail
- ► A promise to "save you hundreds" of dollars inside
- ► Unsolicited credit card applications—extra credit if it is addressed to a minor or to your pet

Procedure:

■ Students will bring in their junk mail collections.

■ They will have kept a record of the number of pieces of mail in each classification of junk mail and the total number of pieces of junk mail that arrived at their homes in the past month.

■ Each student's name will be recorded on chart paper, with the number of pieces of junk mail collected next to it.

Evaluation: Students will group like types of junk mail together.

Grade levels: 4–8

Standards: Thinking and Reasoning, Language Arts

Activity description: Students will examine junk mail and write down terms that are used to try to persuade the reader to take some action.

Preparation and materials:
- Whiteboard or chalkboard to record answers
- Bulletin board area to display junk mail types

Procedure:
- Students will be asked to examine their mail, piece by piece, and find words that are trying to persuade them to believe the advertised product is special and convince them to make a purchase or take some action.

- Suggested words are:
  ► New, free, save, now, real, homemade, sale, easy, taste, hurry, simply, improved, more, better, and an exclamation point

- Students will list the variety of products they are urged to purchase.

- Students will list the variety of actions they are urged to take (e.g., call this number, send this back).

Evaluation: Students will recognize a piece of junk mail and be able to identify its persuasive message.

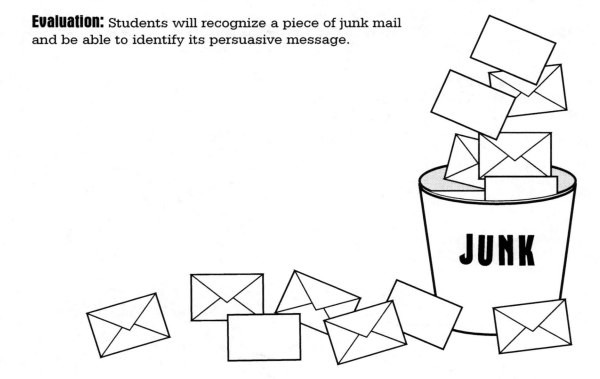

Grade levels: 4–8

Standards: Thinking and Reasoning, Language Arts, Mathematics

Activity description: Students will estimate the number of junk mail items that arrive at their homes each year.

Preparation and materials:

- Figures from previous activity

- Statistics for the number of families represented in your school (the number of households, not number of students)

Procedure:

- Students will add up the total number of junk mail pieces for the class for one month.

- They will calculate the approximate number for the class for one year.

- They will calculate the approximate number for the school population for one year.

- If you know what the population of your community, town, or city is, you can continue with this.

- If possible, get an approximate weight of the junk mail in your class and do the math for that as well.

Evaluation: Students will be able to identify the persuasive techniques used in junk mail and calculate how much they might get each year.

Related Internet Resources:

Nichols, Marcia. *The Junk Mail Explosion: Why You Buy and How Ads Persuade.* 18 October 2003.
<http://www.cbv.ns.ca/sstudies/english/ceclang056.html>

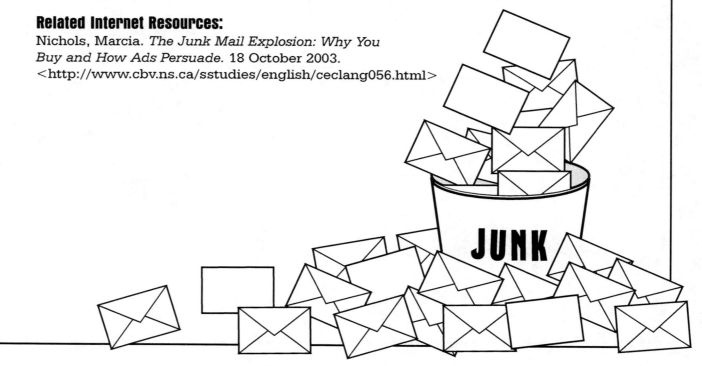

Grade levels: 4–8

Standards: Visual Arts, Thinking and Reasoning, Language Arts

Activity description: Students will talk about different vocabulary terms used in persuasive advertising.

Preparation and materials:

- Make copies of the document "The Language of Persuasion" from the Media Literacy for Health Web site. Eliminate words that you feel are too advanced for your class. Select tab marked "Media Literacy," then select "Basics," then "The Language of Persuasion."
  - ▶ <http://www.nmmlp.org/medialiteracy.htm>

Procedure:

- Distribute the word list to students.

- Talk about these words in class, having a student read the word and the definition.

- Students will draw on personal experience to relate examples to each of these terms.

Evaluation: The students will be able to easily recognize persuasive terms.

Related Internet Resources:

New Mexico Media Literacy Project. *The Language of Persuasion.* 2001. 16 October 2003. <http://www.nmmlp.org/medialiteracy.htm>

Grade levels: 4–8

Standards: Thinking and Reasoning, Language Arts

Activity description: Students will discuss the various meanings of the word violence.

Preparation and materials:
- Dictionary on hand for a student to look up the meaning of violence
  - ► Wordsmyth defines violence this way:
    - Strong, damaging force
    - An act that causes injury or harm
    - The vehement, forceful expression of feeling or use of language
    - Unfair or abusive use of power or force
    - Harm caused by misrepresentation of motive or meaning

- Whiteboard or chalkboard to record student answers

Procedure:
- Ask students to brainstorm. What is the meaning of violence?

- Record all answers.

- Have students name types of violent actions.

- Ask: Is emotional violence as hurtful as physical violence?

- Can emotional violence lead to physical violence?

Evaluation: Students will be aware of the different kinds of violence.

Related Internet Resources:
American Academy of Pediatrics. *Some Things You Should Know About Media Violence and Media Literacy.* 2002. 18 October 2003. <http://www.aap.org/advocacy/childhealthmonth/media.htm>

Center for Media Literacy. *Violence in the Media.* 2002–2003. Center for Media Literacy. 18 October 2003. <http://www.medialit.org/focus/viol_home.html>

Wordsmyth, the Educational Dictionary. 2002. 18 October 2003. <http://www.wordsmyth.net>

Grade levels: 4–8

Standards: Visual Arts, Thinking and Reasoning, Language Arts, Behavioral Studies

Activity description: Students will talk about the violence they witness on TV shows and in cartoons.

Preparation and materials:
- Whiteboard or chalkboard to record student comments

Procedure:
- Ask each student to think about his or her favorite television program.
- Does this show have any violence in it?
- Does it usually display physical violence?
- Does it usually display emotional violence?
- Does it display both kinds of violence?
- When someone gets hurt, how do you feel?

Evaluation: Students will become more aware of the level of violence they are watching.

Television Violence Observation Worksheet

Student Name:_____

Name of Program:_____

Channel:_____   **Length of show:**_____

Directions: As you watch your program, put a check mark in the column next to the violent act each time you see it. Remember, some acts might be repeated.

Act of Violence	Number of Times In Program
Hitting and Punching	
Pushing and Shoving	
Shooting	
Knifing	
Destroying Property	
Put-Downs	
Threats	
Name Calling	
Yelling	

Adapted from *Television and the Lives of Our Children*, Gloria DeGaetano, 1993.
Graphic from: The City of Sacramento Cable Television.
<http://www.ci.west-sacramento.ca.us/community/cable/default.cfm>

Grade levels: 4–8

Standards: Visual Arts, Thinking and Reasoning, Language Arts, Behavioral Studies

Activity description: Students will record the acts of violence in one of their favorite shows.

Preparation and materials:
- Give students the Television Violence Observation worksheet to fill out while they watch one of their favorite TV shows. They will bring the survey back to class for this activity.

Procedure:
- Was the show real or made up?
- Were there a lot of violent acts in the show?
- Were you surprised at the number? Why or why not?
- Which violent action was used the most number of times?
- Were there more violent acts right before a commercial?
- Are there other things going on in the show when the violent act occurs, like music, exaggerated sounds, or bright colors?
- Who committed the most violent acts: men, women, or children?
- Who do the most violent acts harm: men, women, or children?

Evaluation: Students will be more aware of the acts of violence in the shows they watch.

Activity 82   Violence in the Media: TV Shows

Grade levels: 4–8

Standards: Visual Arts, Thinking and Reasoning, Language Arts, Behavioral Studies

Activity description: Children will discuss several of the shows from the previous activity and talk about alternative ways to problem solve.

Preparation and materials:
- Review the list of shows students in your class watched. Pick one or two that were seen by several students.

Procedure:
- Ask the students who watched the show to retell the story. Ask them to specify the incidents that led to the violent action.
- Ask the class if there might have been alternative ways to handle the situation.
- Divide the class into equal size groups.
- Each group will reenact the violent scene with an alternative way to handle the conflict.

Evaluation: Students will be able to suggest a way to avoid violence by choosing a form of conflict resolution for the TV show.

Related Internet Resources:
Media Awareness Network. *Constructive Ways to Handle Conflict.* 14 October 2002. <http://www.media-awareness.ca/english/resources/educational/handouts/violence/ handle_conflict.cfm>

Grade levels: 4–8

Standards: Visual Arts, Thinking and Reasoning, Language Arts, Behavioral Studies

Activity description: Using the same TV shows the class has been discussing, students will discuss the lack of consequences of the violent actions.

Preparation and materials:

- Use several of the shows the children have analyzed for this lesson.

- If you can, videotape several scenes that portray violence.

Procedure:

- The students will watch the scenes with the violence.

- Ask them to note the results and consequences.

  ▶ Would it be like this in real life?

  ▶ Do you see people hurt or bleeding?

  ▶ Does anyone die, and if they do, what happens with them?

  ▶ Is someone blamed for the violence if someone really gets hurt, dies, or damages someone else's property?

  ▶ Who will pay for the damage?

- Is this television portrayal realistic?

Evaluation: Students will be able to recognize that there are usually no realistic consequences for violence in TV shows.

Related Internet Resources:

Media Awareness Network. *Consequences.* 2003 Media Awareness Network. 18 October 2003. <http://www.media-awareness.ca/english/resources/educational/lessons/elementary/violence/ftv_media_violence.cfm>

Media Literacy Clearinghouse. *The Violence Formula: How to Analyze for Violence in TV, Movies and Video.* 2002–2003 Center for Media Literacy. 18 October 2003. <http://www.medialit.org/reading_room/article94.html>

Activity 84   The Good Guys vs. The Bad Guys

Grade levels: 4–8

Standards: Visual Arts, Thinking and Reasoning, Language Arts, Behavioral Studies

Activity description: Students will be asked to consider the stereotypes associated with media violence.

Preparation and materials:
- Whiteboard or chalkboard to record student responses

Procedure:
- Ask students to think about media portrayal of "good guys" and "bad guys."
  - ► Do "good guys" and "bad guys" usually have different physical characteristics? Can you spot the "bad guys" instantly in most shows?
  - ► Do both "good guys" and "bad guys" use violence?
  - ► Is there a difference when the "good guys" or "bad guys" use violence?
  - ► Do they use a different type of violence?
  - ► Do the "bad guys" have families that suffer if something bad happens to them?
  - ► Do "good guys" pay the consequences if they do something violent?

Evaluation: Students will be able to discern the difference in the way violence is portrayed by "good guys" and "bad guys."

Activity 85   Is TV Violence Necessary?

Grade levels: 4–8

Standards: Visual Arts, Thinking and Reasoning, Language Arts, Behavioral Studies

Activity description: Students will examine the shows they watched and rated at home to determine if the violence enhanced the show.

Preparation and materials:
- Use the shows the students rated in the previous activities.

Procedure:
- Ask students to consider:
  - ► What role does violence play in the program?
  - ► Would there be any show without the violent conflict?
  - ► Does the violence just add excitement to the show?
  - ► Do you think the violence was necessary in the particular situation?
  - ► Would you watch the show if it were not as violent as it is?

Evaluation: Students will be able to evaluate the use of violence in television programming.

Related Internet Resources:
Iowa State University. *The Impact of Entertainment Media Violence on Children and Families.* Last update 02/04/02. 14 October 2003. <http://www.extension.iastate.edu/families/media/index.html>

VIDEO GAME WORKSHEET

Name: _____

1. How much time do you spend playing video games?

1 hour per week or less
1–3 hours per week
3–6 hours per week
6–10 hours per week
10 hours or more per week

2. What are your three favorite games? Why do you like them? Do they contain violence?

Name of Game	Reasons for liking it	Contains violence

3. What types of games are they?

4. Do you usually play video games alone, or with friends?

5. How long do you usually play a game before you want to quit?

6. Do you have trouble leaving the game?

7. Do you ever get angry or frustrated when playing a video game?

8. If so, what do you do about it?

Grade levels: 4–8

Standards: Visual Arts, Thinking and Reasoning, Language Arts, Behavioral Studies

Activity description: Students will examine the appeal of video games.

Preparation and materials:
- Students will bring in the completed Video Game Worksheet.

Procedure:
- Before students share their Video Game Worksheets, ask them why they like video games.
  - ▶ Answers will probably include:
    - There is challenge, control, and eventual mastery over the game.
    - The game provides instant gratification and reinforcement.
    - The game is a great escape from the real world.

- Invite students to share their Video Game Worksheets.

Evaluation:
Students will explore the appeal of video games and compare how much they use them with other students in the class.

Related Internet Resources:
Media Awareness Network. *Video Games.* 14 October 2003.
<http://www.media-awareness.ca/english/resources/research_documents/studies/video_games/vgc_preferences.cfm>

Grade levels: 4–8

Standards: Visual Arts, Thinking and Reasoning, Language Arts, Behavioral Studies

Activity description: Students will be able to describe an ad that uses a celebrity and analyze why the celebrity is picked for that particular product.

Preparation and materials:

- Bring in copies of ads that students will recognize.

- Cover the text so students cannot see what the actual advertised product is.

Procedure:

- Discuss celebrities with the class.

- Record the list of student's favorite celebrities, including those from sports, movies, video, and television.

- Divide the class into small discussion groups.

- Distribute an advertisement to each group of students.

- Have students in each group discuss:

  - ▶ How do the celebrities look in the ad?
  - ▶ What are they doing?
  - ▶ Which company made the ad?
  - ▶ Where is the celebrity looking?
  - ▶ What are the celebrities wearing?
  - ▶ What makes the ad appealing?
  - ▶ Is there anyone else in the ad?
  - ▶ What is shown?
  - ▶ What is left out?

Evaluation: Students will be able to identify the role of celebrities in advertising.

Grade levels: 4–8

Standards: Thinking and Reasoning, Language Arts

Activity description: Students will be able to identify persuasive ads by recognizing the vocabulary used in them.

Preparation and materials:
- Display your collection of persuasive print advertisements. These can be obtained from many magazines, especially *Sports Illustrated for Kids* and magazines like *House and Garden* that often have ads for household products.

Procedure:
- Students will examine ads and point out vocabulary words that are trying to persuade the audience to do or buy something.

- Have them look for these persuasive words:
  - ▶ suddenly, miracle, now, magic, announcing, offer, introducing, quick, improvement, easy, amazing, wanted, sensational, challenge, remarkable, compare, revolutionary, bargain, startling, hurry, free offer, new, revolutionary, quick, advice to, suddenly, easy, the truth about, wanted, last chance, challenge, it's here, introducing, just arrived

Evaluation: Students will be able to readily recognize persuasive words in ads.

Related Internet Resources:
Flaningam, J. *Critical Consumerism*. 2001–2002. Oakland Unified School District. 17 October 2003. <http://www210.pair.com/udticg/lessonplans/consumerism/worksheet8.htm>

Grade levels: 4–8

Standards: Thinking and Reasoning, Language Arts

Activity description: Students will examine ads that sell ideas, lifestyles, and images, rather than a tangible product.

Preparation and materials:

■ Collect and display several advertisements that sell an image, an idea, or a lifestyle and have the students examine them.

Procedure:

■ Divide students into groups.

■ Each group will examine one ad that you have selected.

■ Students will evaluate:

▶ What is the first thing you notice in the ad?

▶ What information is given about the specific product?

▶ What seems to be the most important thing in the image?

▶ Is there a lifestyle or fantasy being promoted?

▶ What is the message of the ad?

■ Stress the fact that very little information is offered about the product. Through the creation of an image or a fantasy, the consumer is led to believe that the product is the key to obtaining that lifestyle or fantasy.

■ Ask students to identify ads that they have seen that do the same thing.

Evaluation: Students will identify that the connection to a product is often a connection with the fantasy the ad creates.

Grade levels: 4–8

Standards: Thinking and Reasoning, Language Arts, Visual Arts

Activity description: Students will create an ad for a product that uses an image, lifestyle, or a fantasy instead of focusing on the product.

Preparation and materials:
- Poster paper for student ads

Procedure:
- Students will each select a product that they use.

- They will create a persuasive ad for the product by creating an ad that focuses on an image, a lifestyle, or a fantasy rather than the product itself.

- Some ideas:
    - ▶ Wearing a particular brand of sneaker will make you better at a sport
    - ▶ Eating a particular food will make you prettier/more handsome
    - ▶ Eating a particular food will make you smarter
    - ▶ Eating at a certain restaurant will make you thinner

Evaluation: Students will demonstrate their knowledge of persuasive advertising by creating a fantasy image to sell a product.

Grade levels: 4–8

Standards: Thinking and Reasoning, Language Arts, Visual Arts

Activity description: Students will understand the five basic types of advertising, and their similarities and differences.

Preparation and materials:

■ Collect print advertisements that fall into the following five categories:

▸ **Traditional**—The product or service is clearly identified, and a call to action is made (buy this product, use this service, call this telephone number).

▸ **Image**—The company or organization seeks to be associated with a certain feeling, image, or cause. It is important to note that products or services are not always featured in image advertising.

▸ **Product placement**—A company pays for a product or message to be featured in an entertainment vehicle, such as a movie or music video.

▸ **Event sponsorship**—A sponsor's name is displayed prominently at event venues, on ticket stubs, or other items associated with a special event.

▸ **Celebrity endorsement**—A well-known person is paid to promote a product or service.

Procedure:

■ Discuss and define the five categories of advertisements shown above. Have advertisements prepared for students to evaluate.

■ Students will look at each ad and determine which category the ad endorsement belongs to.

■ Have students talk about the particular celebrity and whether he or she is involved in the sport or product, or if it is just a use of stardom to create an association with a product.

Evaluation: Students will be more aware that celebrity endorsement does not necessarily mean that a celebrity likes or uses the product, and their impulse to buy the product themselves might be their response to the celebrity rather than the product.

Related Internet Resources:

Center for Substance Abuse Prevention. *It's an Ad Ad Ad Ad World.*" 2002 May. PC World. 18 October 2003. <http://www.pcworld.com/resource/printable/article0,aid,86929,00.asp>

Grade levels: 4–8

Standards: Thinking and Reasoning, Language Arts, Visual Arts

Activity description: Students will track TV, radio, and newspaper advertisements for celebrity endorsements and talk about the effectiveness of this type of advertisement.

Preparation and materials:
- Prepare copies of Celebrity Endorsement Worksheet.

Procedure:
- Students will track TV, radio, newspaper, and any other advertisements they see that contain celebrity endorsements for one weekend.

- Students will bring their worksheets to class.

- Students will share information.

- Categorize celebrities according to profession and interests such as sports, movies and television.

Evaluation:
Students will demonstrate recognition of the fact that celebrities are often used to endorse products.

CELEBRITY PRODUCT ENDORSEMENT WORKSHEET

Name: _____

Product	Celebrity	Where the Ad Is Found	Message to Kids

Grade levels: 4–8

Standards: Thinking and Reasoning, Language Arts, Visual Arts

Activity description: Students will deconstruct celebrity ads.

Preparation and materials:
■ Use worksheet analysis from previous lesson.

Procedure:
■ Students will discuss:
- ► Reasons for a selecting a particular celebrity
- ► Whether the celebrity endorsement actually ties in with the celebrity's personal preferences
- ► Whether the endorsement entices the student to ask for a particular product
- ► Why the celebrity endorsement might appeal to students and encourage them to purchase or ask for a particular product

■ Ask students if these partnerships between product and personality create misleading or false impressions.

■ How might they do this?

■ If the person buys a product that is endorsed by a celebrity that he or she likes or respects, is the buyer supporting the product or the celebrity?

Evaluation: Students will be able to question celebrity endorsements and recognize that they are often just a technique to sell a product.

Related Internet Resources:
Office of NY State Attorney General Eliot Spitzer. *What's in a Non-Profit's Name?* 2002 OAG. 18 October 2003. <http://www.oag.state.ny.us/press/reports/nonprofit/full_text.html>

Schrank, Jeffrey. *The Module on Advertising Claims*. Center for the Study of Commercialism, Washington D.C. 16 October 2003.
<http://home.olemiss.edu/~egjbp/comp/ad-claims.html>

Consumersunion.org. *Selling America's Kids: Commercial Pressures on Kids of the 90's. Celebrity Endorsements.* 1998. Consumer's Union. 16 October 2003.
<http://www.consumersunion.org/other/sellingkids/celebrity.htm>

Grade levels: 4–8

Standards: Thinking and Reasoning, Language Arts, Visual Arts, Art Connection

Activity description: Students will create an ad using their favorite celebrity.

Preparation and materials:
- Poster paper for students

Procedure:
- Each student will pick a celebrity.

- Each student will pick a product he or she wants the celebrity to endorse.

- Students will create a poster with an advertisement using their celebrity and product.
    - They will need to consider the basic elements of an ad.
    - They will use persuasive writing to try to convince the viewer to buy the product.

Evaluation: Posters will reveal student comprehension of persuasive advertising.

Grade levels: 4–8

Standards: Thinking and Reasoning, Language Arts, Visual Arts

Activity description: Students will examine magazines and evaluate the percentage of ads in them.

Preparation and materials:

- Ask students to bring in magazines that they subscribe to.

- Collect copies of:

  - Grades 1–2: *Highlights, Cricket, Ranger Rick, Your Big Backyard, Cobblestone, Cricket, Spider,* and any other appropriate and available magazines.

  - Grades 3–6: *Sports Illustrated for Kids, Nintendo, American Girl, National Geographic for Kids, Nickelodeon, Muse,* and any other appropriate and available magazines.

  - Grades 7–8: *Teen, Cosmo Girl, Teen People, Seventeen, Sports Illustrated,* and any other appropriate and available magazines.

Procedure:

- Display copies of each magazine on tables and allow the students to examine them.

- Students will complete a magazine evaluation worksheet for at least one magazine.

- Discuss findings with the class:

  - Which magazines have ads? Why?

  - Which magazines don't have advertisements? Why not?

  - Do certain magazines only advertise their own products?

  - Who publishes the magazines?

  - Who pays for the creation of the magazines?

Evaluation: Students will be able to recognize that some magazines are published by non-profit educational organizations and do not offer advertising, while the commercial publications are mostly ads.

Related Internet Resources:

Association of Educational Publishers. *Flip for Magazines. The Magazine Connection.* 2002. Association of Educational Publisher. 17 October 2003. <http://www.childmagmonth.org/connection/index.html>

Grade levels: 4–8

Standards: Thinking and Reasoning, Language Arts, Visual Arts

Activity description: Students will examine specific commercial children's magazines and the ads that appear in them.

Preparation and materials:
- Copies for each student or group of students of commercial magazines

Procedure:
- Divide students into groups.
- Each group will examine a magazine and the ads in it.
- Each group will complete a magazine ad worksheet.
- Students will discuss their findings.

Evaluation: Students will be able to deconstruct magazine ads.

MAGAZINE AD WORKSHEET

Name: _____

Examine the magazine advertisement you have been assigned to evaluate. Complete the information below.

Title of magazine:_____

Publication date: _____

Cost of magazine: _____

General subject of magazine: _____

What type of company publishes the magazine? _____

Who is the target audience? _____

What types of products are advertised? _____

Who will make money from this ad? _____

Is the ad believable? _____

How does the image or picture make the product more appealing?

_____

Does the text support the message from the image?

_____

Is there a hidden message? _____

What is it? _____

Grade levels: 4–8

Standards: Thinking and Reasoning, Language Arts, Visual Arts

Activity description: Students will create a classroom magazine.

Preparation and materials:

- Get copies of classroom magazines for your class to browse.

Procedure:

- Brainstorm to choose a subject for the magazine.
  - ► Sports
  - ► Fashion
  - ► Reading
  - ► Particular curriculum subject (e.g., Ancient Civilizations, Plate Tectonics, Butterflies)

- Brainstorm to select a name for the magazine.

- Divide students into groups that will each be responsible for a certain task.
  - ► Cover
  - ► Contents page
  - ► Feature articles
  - ► Editorials/Advice columns
  - ► Advertisements

Evaluation: Students will begin to create a classroom magazine.

Related Internet Resources:

San Jose, Christine. *Teacher to Teacher: Creating a Classroom Magazine.* 2002. Ohio Literacy Resource Center. 17 October 2003. <http://literacy.kent.edu/Oasis/Pubs/0300-5.htm>

Olson, Kendra. *Create Your Own Magazine.* Media Literacy Clearinghouse. 17 October 2003. <http://www.med.sc.edu:1081/createmag.htm>

Activity 101　Classroom Magazine: Cover Group I

Grade levels: 4–8

Standards: Language Arts, Visual Arts, Working with Others

Activity description: Students will create a cover for their classroom magazine.

Preparation and materials:
- Have many examples of magazines available for students to examine.

Procedure:
- Students in the cover group will:
  - ▶ Look at the cover designs of magazines
  - ▶ Determine the target audience for the classroom magazine
  - ▶ Decide on the layout for the classroom magazine cover
  - ▶ Divide the tasks and begin the creation of the cover

Evaluation: Students will work cooperatively to create a cover for a class magazine.

Activity 102　Classroom Magazine: Cover Group II

Grade levels: 4–8

Standards: Language Arts, Visual Arts, Working with Others, Technology

Activity description: Students will create a magazine cover using a desktop publishing program or a word processing program.

Preparation and materials:
- Review desktop publishing or word processing software with students.

Procedure:
- Students will create a magazine cover using a word processing program such as Microsoft® Word®.
  - ▶ They can use WordArt® to create the masthead for the magazine title and insert graphic images or scanned images and text boxes to complete the cover.

Evaluation: A magazine cover will be created using computer software.

Related Internet Resources:
If you have Microsoft® PictureIt.®, this is an excellent tutorial for a magazine cover.
Lycos. *Creating a Magazine Cover*. 2002. 17 October 2003.
<http://howto.lycos.com/lycos/step/1,,6+33+104+23054+11982,00.html>

Activity 103 | Magazine: Creating the Contents, Feature Articles, and Editorials

Grade levels: 4–8

Standards: Language Arts, Visual Arts, Working with Others

Activity description: Students will work in groups to create a page for the magazine contents, feature articles, editorials, and advice columns.

Preparation and materials:
- In deciding what is to be included in the magazine, students need to ask:
  - ► Does this meet our magazine's goal?
  - ► Does the product measure up to the quality expected?

Procedure:
- Students in each group will work together and determine the contents of their assignment.
- They will create their pages using paper and pencils, crayons, or computer software.

Evaluation: Each group will work cooperatively to finish its task.

Activity 104 | Magazine: Advertisements

Grade levels: 4–8

Standards: Language Arts, Visual Arts, Working with Others

Activity description: Students in the advertising group will create the ads for their classroom magazine.

Preparation and materials:
- Students will need to decide what advertisements are going to be published in their magazine.
  - ► Is the ad consistent with the theme of the magazine?
  - ► Will the ad promote the contents of the magazine?
  - ► Is the ad appropriate for the magazine's target audience?

Procedure:
- Students will work together to determine the wording for each advertisement.
- Students will create all original works, including the photographs, drawings, slogans, and perhaps even the products!
- For each ad created, they will need to complete an advertisement worksheet.

Evaluation: Students will work together to create effective, persuasive ads for their classroom magazine.

CREATE A MAGAZINE AD WORKSHEET

Name: _____

Product	Basic Message
Visual Image	**Catchy Words**
Target Audience	**What Action Should the Reader Take?**
Size of Ad	**Persuasion Techniques**

Grade levels: 4–8

Standards: Language Arts, Visual Arts, Working with Others

Activity description: Students will be introduced to a copy of the local newspaper and learn about the parts of a newspaper.

Preparation and materials:

- Contact your local newspaper and request enough copies for each student (or let them work in pairs) in your classroom for one week.

- Find out if your local newspaper is associated with the Newspapers in Education program.

- You'll need a whieboard or chalkboard to record student responses.

- Read the Internet article *It's News to Me: Teaching Kids about the Newspaper* <http://www.education-world.com/a_lesson/lesson140.shtml>.

Procedure:

- Ask students what they know about the newspaper.
  - ▸ What are the different sections?
  - ▸ What can you find in each section?
  - ▸ With the newspapers in the children's hands, have them look at it together.
    - • With younger students, you might want to move the lesson to the floor so it is easier for them to handle the pages.
    - • Go over the front page with them. Point to and name the different parts of the front page.
- A great interactive site for them to look at together, or to use for your guidance, can be found at Education Resources "Getting to Know the Front Page" from the StarTribune <http://www.startribune.com/education/know.shtml>.
  - ▸ Demonstrate how to follow an article from one column to the next and from the front page to the jump page (the page on which an article is continued from the front page).

Evaluation: Students will be able to look at a newspaper and understand the composition of the front page.

Related Internet Resources:

Noll, Melody. *Exploring a Newspaper. The Language Fun Farm.* 17 October 2003. <http://www.teflfarm.com/teachers/qualifications/lesson_plans/exploring.htm>

Education World. *It's News to Me: Teaching Kids about the Newspaper.* 1996–2002. 17 October 2003. <http://www.education-world.com/a_lesson/lesson140.shtml>

Activity 107   Newspapers: Beyond the Front Page

Grade levels: 4–8

Standards: Language Arts, Visual Arts

Activity description: Students will continue navigating the newspaper.

Preparation and materials:
- A copy of the local newspaper for every student

Procedure:
- Briefly review parts of the front page.

- Have students explore additional sections of the paper along with you. Be sure to point out the:
    - *Indexes*: General index on page one or two; index in the classified ad section; indexes that may appear in individual sections.
    - *Section heads*: The section head at the top of the first page of a section, listing the title of the section and any special features.
    - *Page heads*: Headers at the top of each page indicating the type of news on that page, such as local news, education, or editorial.
    - *Anchored features*: Features placed in the same place in every issue of the paper. The weather map, comics, and editorial section may be anchored in your local newspaper.

- Be sure to direct students to advertisements in the paper!

Evaluation: Students will become familiar with the contents of a newspaper.

Activity 108   Newspapers: Messages with Different Purposes

Grade levels: 4–8

Standards: Language Arts, Visual Arts, Working with Others, Technology

Activity description: Students will understand the several types of media messages that appear in a newspaper.

Preparation and materials:
- A copy of the local newspaper for every student

Procedure:
- Lead students through the newspaper and have them notice the different types of messages that appear:
    - Information
    - Entertainment
    - Persuasion

- Students will look at the paper in teams and complete a Newspaper Message Worksheet.

Evaluation: Students can identify the type of messages in a newspaper.

NEWSPAPER MESSAGE WORKSHEET

Name: _____

Look through the newspaper and find examples of the different parts of a newspaper that are in one of these categories: **INFORMATION, PERSUASION,** or **ENTERTAINMENT**. Please find three of each category.

Newspaper Article	Page	Category	Reason you put it in this category

Grade levels: 4 and 5

Standards: Language Arts, Visual Arts

Activity description: Students will locate specific items in a newspaper that are listed on the Scavenger Hunt worksheet.

Preparation and materials:

■ Newspapers, scissors, glue, and poster board for each group

Procedure:

■ Students will search through the newspaper and locate the listed items.

■ Students will cut out each item and glue it onto poster board.

■ They will check off each item as they locate it.

Evaluation: Students will be able to identify general newspaper items.

NEWSPAPER SCAVENGER HUNT

Name: _____

Locate the following items in the newspaper. Check them off as you find them. Cut each one out and paste it on the poster board.

☐ something to drink   ☐ something to eat

☐ something to play with   ☐ something to ride in or on

☐ something to wear   ☐ something alive

☐ something hot   ☐ something cold

☐ something that's big   ☐ something that makes you frown

☐ something that makes you smile   ☐ a store

☐ something that uses electricity   ☐ a number

☐ a male

☐ a female

☐ a store

☐ big black print

☐ teeny tiny print

Grade levels: 4–8

Standards: Language Arts, Visual Arts, Mathematics

Activity description: Students will locate specific mathematical items in a newspaper.

Preparation and materials:
- Newspapers, scissors, glue, and poster board for each group

Procedure:
- Students will search through the newspaper and locate the listed items.
- Students will cut out each item and glue it onto poster board.
- They will check off each item as they locate it.

Evaluation: Students will be able to identify general newspaper items.

MATH SCAVENGER HUNT

Name: _____

Locate the following items in the newspaper. Check them off as you find find them. Cut each one out and paste it on the poster board.

☐ number over 1,000	☐ number less than 10
☐ numeral between 10 and 100	☐ telephone number
☐ address	☐ Roman numeral
☐ number written in words	☐ radio call number
☐ TV channel number	☐ ID of any kind
☐ temperature	☐ rectangle
☐ circle	☐ triangle
☐ fraction	☐ decimal but not money
☐ percent	☐ an age
☐ zip code	☐ date

Grade levels: 4–8

Standards: Language Arts, Visual Arts

Activity description: The students will examine a news article in detail.

Preparation and materials:

■ Each student will have a copy of the local newspaper.

Procedure:

■ Select a news article that many students seem interested in.

■ Have them think about what makes this interesting or a good article.

■ Brainstorm to pinpoint the elements of a good news article.

▶ The categories of good reporting are who, what, when, where, why, and how.

▶ Have students identify these elements in the selected news article.

■ Who is the target audience of this news article?

■ Who is scripting the message?

■ Why is it written this way?

Evaluation: Students will be able to identify the critical components of a news article.

Grade levels: 4–8

Standards: Language Arts, Visual Arts

Activity description: Students will create a news article.

Preparation and materials:

Procedure:

- Students will write strong headline phrases for their news article.

- They will write their by-lines.

- They will create their lead paragraphs which offer information to the reader and answers the questions:

  ► Who?
    • Write the name of the person the news is about.

  ► What?
    • Explain in a short sentence what occurred.

  ► Where?
    • Write a phrase that describes the place where the news occurred.

  ► When?
    • Write the day, date, and time of day.

  ► Why?
    • Tell why the news happened.

- Write supportive paragraphs, including eyewitness descriptions of the incident.

- Close the article by indicating how the news might affect other people.

Evaluation: Students will create a well-written, informative news article about something of interest to the class.

Related Internet Resources:

Global SchoolNet Foundation. *Newsday*. 2001. 17 October 2003.
<http://www.gsn.org/project/newsday/index.html>

Education Resources. *You Can Write a News Story*. Star Tribune. 17 October 2003.
<http://www.startribune.com/education/writing.shtml>

Rusnak, B.S. Ed., Stephanie M. *Media Awareness Network. Formula for a Well-Written News Article*. 27 October 2002. <http://www.media-awareness.ca/english/resources/educational/handouts/broadcast_news/news_article_formula.cfm>

Grade levels: 4–8

Standards: Language Arts, Visual Arts

Activity description: Students will examine feature articles in a newspaper.

Preparation and materials:

- A copy of the local newspaper for each student

- Whiteboard or chalkboard

Procedure:

- Ask students to name the components of a feature article as compared to a news article.

    ▶ Subject matter is less timely.

    ▶ Leads can be creative rather than just news leads.

    ▶ Use of many sources, quotes, creative endings, and descriptive writing.

    ▶ Feature subject might not impact anyone.

Evaluation: Students will be able to identify a feature article.

Related Internet Resources:

USnews.com. *Writing News Features and Sidebars.* 17 October 2003.
<http://www.usnewsclassroom.com/resources/activities/act011203.html>

Global SchoolNet Foundation. *Newsday: Interview/Feature Article.* 2001.
17 October 2003. <http://www.gsn.org/project/newsday/lp2/index.html>

Activity 117 — Newspapers: The Interview for Writing a Feature Article

Grade levels: 4–8

Standards: Language Arts, Visual Arts, Behavioral Studies

Activity description: Students will conduct an interview with someone in the school to create a feature article.

Preparation and materials:
- The class will determine the target audience (students, parents, the community).

Procedure:
- The class will be divided into teams.
- Each team will pick or be assigned a person in the school to interview.
- Students will take notes and write down direct quotes from the interview.
- Students will have a clear idea of the nature of the article by thinking about what their groups want to feature.
- Student preparation will include:
  - ▶ Prepare a question to get the person to describe something you want to know.
  - ▶ Prepare a question to get the person to describe what he or she did in the situation being covered.
  - ▶ Prepare a question to find out how the interviewee feels.
  - ▶ Prepare a question to prompt the person to describe the effects it has had on him or her.

Evaluation: The student interview will result in the gathering of enough information to write a well-constructed feature article.

Activity 118 — Writing the Feature Article After the Interview

Grade levels: 4–8

Standards: Language Arts, Visual Arts, Behavioral Studies

Activity description: Students will write a feature article.

Preparation and materials:
- Students will have notes from the interview conducted in previous activity.

Procedure:
- Students will write an introduction to the interview.
- Students will create a sentence to introduce the person interviewed, including name, age, and description.
- They will supply details about the interview: place, time, year, and season.
- Students will use direct quotes where they are appropriate.
- They will describe the tone the person used in answering the questions.
- Students will wrap up the article with a conclusion that includes a reflection of what they learned.
- Students will create an appropriate headline and insert their by-lines.
- Students will include a photograph of the interviewee if they can.

Evaluation: Students will create an interesting and informative feature article.

Activity 119   Newspapers: Classified Ads

Grade levels: 4–8

Standards: Language Arts, Visual Arts, Behavioral Studies

Activity description: Students will examine the classified ad section of the local newspaper.

Preparation and materials:
- Whiteboard or chalkboard to record student responses

Procedure:
- Allow students time to look over the classified ads.
- Ask students to categorize the different types of ads they find and record their answers.
  - ▶ Help wanted
  - ▶ Items for sale
  - ▶ Automotive
  - ▶ Houses for sale
  - ▶ Apartments for rent
  - ▶ Services available
- Identify the persuasive terminology used in the ads.
- For each advertisement, answer the following:
  - ▶ What product is being sold?
  - ▶ How would you generally describe the ad?
  - ▶ What items, if any, are being associated with the product?
  - ▶ What is the message of the ad?

Evaluation: Students will become familiar with the persuasive writing used in classified ads.

Activity 120   Newspapers: Create a Classified Ad

Grade levels: 4–8

Standards: Language Arts, Visual Arts, Behavioral Studies

Activity description: Students will create a classified ad.

Preparation and materials:
- Display examples of different types of classified ads.

Procedure:
- Students will pick the type of ad they want to create from the following list:
  - ▶ Help wanted
  - ▶ Item for sale
  - ▶ Services available
- Each student will create an appropriate, persuasive ad.
- Students will use Ad Worksheets.

Evaluation: Students will understand the elements of a good classified ad.

Classified: Help Wanted

Grade levels: 4–8

Standards: Language Arts, Visual Arts, Behavioral Studies

Activity description: Students will create a help wanted ad.

Preparation and materials:

■ Bring in and display a large selection of help wanted newspaper ads.

Procedure:

■ Students will determine the criteria for a good newspaper help wanted ad.

■ Students will examine a group of help wanted ads.

■ Brainstorm with students to see what jobs they can advertise. It might be fun to write a help wanted ad for a school principal or a classroom teacher.

■ Students will work in pairs to write a help wanted ad.

■ Be sure they include:
  ▶ Job Summary
  ▶ Duties and Responsibilities
  ▶ Qualifications

■ Keep the ad simple, direct, and to the point.

■ Give specifics.

■ Be sure students include the information on how to apply.

Evaluation: Students will create a clear and appropriate classified ad for a job.

Internet Resources:

The Daily World. *Writing Your Own Classified Ad.* 2002. 15 October 2003.
<http://www.thedailyworld.com/classifieds/ad_form.html>

Write 101.com. *My Ads Aren't Working Quick Tips.* 2000. 15 October 2003.
<http://www.write101.com/20octadv.htm>

Classified Ad—Help Wanted

Name: _____

Decide on a job you want to advertise in the local newspaper. Write an ad for that job to be printed in the Help Wanted section.

Help Wanted

Job Summary
Duties and Responsibilities
Qualifications, Special Skills, and Experience Required
Wages, Benefits, Security, and Hours
Where and How to Apply

Classified Services

Classified Ad—Services Wanted

Name: _____

Decide on a service you want to advertise in the local newspaper. Write an ad for that service to be printed in the Services Available section.

Services Wanted

Services Available
Description of the Service
Qualifications and Experience
Benefits of Using Service
How to Contact the Service Provider

Activity 124   Item For Sale Ads

Grade levels: 4–8

Standards: Language Arts, Visual Arts, Behavioral Studies

Activity description: Students will write a classified ad for an item for sale.

Preparation and materials:
- Newspaper ads
- Item For Sale Worksheet

Procedure:
- Students will decide what items they want to advertise.
- Following clear guidelines, students will create a for sale ad that will include:
  - ▶ Type of item (car, furniture, computer)
  - ▶ Sale date
  - ▶ Price
  - ▶ Make and model
  - ▶ Size and color
  - ▶ New or used
  - ▶ Delivery options
  - ▶ Seller's information

Evaluation: Students will write a persuasive for sale ad.

Classified Ad – Item For Sale

Name: _____

Decide on an item you want to advertise in the local newspaper. Write an ad for that item to be printed in the Items For Sale section.

Item For Sale

Services Available
Description of the Item
Special Features of Item
Benefits of Item
Asking Price and How to Contact the Seller

Grade levels: 4–8

Standards: Language Arts, Visual Arts, Behavioral Studies, Thinking and Reasoning

Activity description: Students will compare a news article in several papers, identifying the similarities and differences.

Preparation and materials:

- Collect news articles from several different newspapers that deal with the same event.

- Prepare copies of each for the groups of students.

Procedure:

- Divide the class into small groups.

- Distribute a set of news articles to each group.

- Students will read the articles and compare and note their differences and similarities in:
  - ▸ The presentation of information
  - ▸ The point of view of the author or publisher
  - ▸ The social, political, economic, and historic facts

- Students will discuss why there might be differences.

- Ask students if they think that one particular article was more accurate than another and why.

Evaluation: Students will understand that newspapers are scripted to relay the news from the point of view of the writer and publisher.

Related Internet Resources:

Newspapers in Education. *Curriculum Materials*. 2002. 16 October 2003.
<http://www.fredericksburg.com/nie/content/Curriculum>

Activity 127   News Stories: What Is on the Front Page?

Grade levels: 4–8

Standards: Language Arts, Visual Arts, Behavioral Studies, Thinking and Reasoning

Activity description: Students will collect and read the front page of a local newspaper for one week and track the types of articles that appear there.

Preparation and materials:
- Copies of the front page of a local newspaper, collected for one week

Procedure:
- Divide the students into groups.
- Each group will examine the stack of front pages from the local newspaper.
- Students will divide the subjects of the front page news stories into groups and see if there is a pattern to the types of story featured on the front page.
- Class will discuss findings and understand why certain articles are placed on the front page and why others are found on interior pages.
- Class will track the types of articles.
  - ▶ Is the most important article on the front? Why?
  - ▶ What article is given the most space? Why?
  - ▶ What type of subject is given the most coverage? Why?

Evaluation: Students will see that articles of importance vary, depending on the type of newspaper and the opinions of the editors and writers.

Activity 128   Newspaper or Television? Which News Is Accurate?

Grade levels: 4–8

Standards: Language Arts, Visual Arts, Behavioral Studies, Thinking and Reasoning

Activity description: The students will compare a news story as told by a local newspaper with a news story told by a local television news station.

Preparation and materials:
- Select a current events story.
- Prepare class copies of the newspaper coverage of that subject.
- Tape segments of the television news that feature that story.

Procedure:
- The class will look over a newspaper story about a specific subject or event.
- The class will look at a tape of the local news covering the same story.
- Discuss:
  - ▶ Which version is the most reliable?
  - ▶ Which does a better job?
  - ▶ How do you know which one to believe if they are not the same?

Evaluation: Members of the class will be able to decide which news coverage they feel is more effective—newspaper or television.

Grade levels: 4–8

Standards: Language Arts, Visual Arts, Behavioral Studies, Thinking and Reasoning

Activity description: Students will examine local and national newspapers and categorize the front page news articles.

Preparation and materials:

- Collect the front pages from a local and a national newspaper for one week.

- Make copies for six groups of students.

Procedure:

- Divide the class into six groups.

- Distribute a set of front pages to each group.

- Students will examine the front page headlines and stories.

- Students will categorize the stories:

  - ▶ Good news

  - ▶ National news

  - ▶ Local news

- Students will track how many times a particular news item appears during the week and determine if the position on the front page is different than in previous days.

- Group discussion questions:

  - ▶ Does the news article lose impact if it appears for more than one day?

  - ▶ What is the point of carrying the coverage for more than one day?

  - ▶ Do both newspapers cover the same news stories?

  - ▶ If they do, is the coverage the same?

  - ▶ What is different?

  - ▶ Does the article have pictures?
    - • If so, what impact do the pictures have on your perception of the article?

  - ▶ Does the headline influence your opinion of the story before you even read it?

  - ▶ Does placement on the page influence your reading the story?

  - ▶ Do the articles present a personal perspective?

Evaluation: Students will observe the construction of the front page of a newspaper and evaluate it for content and bias.

THE FRONT PAGE

Name: _____

Newspaper	Local	National Newspaper	Target Audience	Pictures? Y/N
Name of newspaper				
Date of publication				
Headline article – Day 1				
Headline article – Day 2				
Headline article – Day 3				
Headline article – Day 4				
Headline article – Day 5				
Headline article – Day 6				
Headline article – Day 7				
Other articles:				
Day 1				
Day 2				
Day 3				
Day 4				
Day 5				
Day 6				
Day 7				

Grade levels: 4–8

Standards: Language Arts, Thinking and Reasoning

Activity description: Students will discuss the results of the Radio Frequency Worksheet.

Preparation and materials:
■ Copy a Radio Frequency Worksheet for each student and have each student fill it out.

Procedure:
■ Students will share their information from the worksheet.

■ Discuss the answers.

■ Rate each question and try to get a class average.

■ Discuss the class's listening habits.
   ► Does everyone fall into the same target audience category?

Evaluation: Students will be able to determine why they listen to the radio.

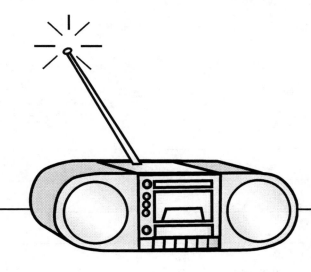

RADIO FREQUENCY WORKSHEET

Name: _____

Directions: Either circle the answer that is right for you or fill in the blanks with information. There is no one right answer.

1. How often do you listen to the radio?

    every day   once a week   hardly ever

2. Where do you listen to the radio?

    in the car   in my room   in other parts of the house

3. You listen to the radio to hear . . .

    music   news   talk shows

4. How many hours a day do you listen to the radio? _____

5. Do other members of your family listen to the radio? _____

6. What is the target audience of the station you listen to most frequently?_____

7. Does your station have advertisements? _____

8. How many advertisements air in half an hour? _____

9. Name some products advertised on your station.

    _____

    _____

    _____

    _____

10. Do you listen to radio newscasts? _____

11. What news is presented?

    local news   national news   international news   weather   sports

Grade levels: 4–8

Standards: Language Arts, Thinking and Reasoning

Activity description: Using the answers from the previous lesson and worksheet, track the type of advertisements on a particular radio station.

Preparation and materials:
- Whiteboard or chalkboard for recording answers

Procedure:
- Track the types of advertisements heard on the radio for one week.
  - ▶ Be sure to keep them separated by station.

- Ask students to find a pattern in the answers.
  - ▶ Does the target audience have any influence on the type of product advertised?
  - ▶ Do certain products appear regularly on certain stations and not at all on others?
  - ▶ How many minutes/seconds do the ads take?
  - ▶ Are the ads as appealing as the ones on television or in a magazine?
  - ▶ What are some of the differences between ads on television and ads on the radio?
    - • Are the radio ads as effective as television ads?

Evaluation: Students will be able recognize the connection between target audience and advertisements.

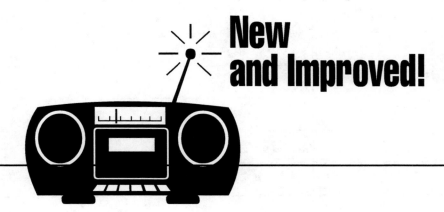

RADIO ADS

New and Improved!

Name: _____

Product Advertised	Time of Advertisement	Target Audience	Does It Appeal to You?	Date

Grade levels: 4–8

Standards: Language Arts, Thinking and Reasoning

Activity description: Students will listen to a radio news program and extract necessary information from it.

Preparation and materials:
- Tape several radio newsbreaks.
    - ▶ Use at least one local and one national news segment.
    - ▶ Try to use news clips that are also featured on television news.
- Copy a Radio Broadcast News Worksheet for each student.

Procedure:
- Each student will have a Radio News Broadcast Worksheet for each news clip.
- Play the first news broadcast for the class.
    - ▶ Go over any questions students might have concerning the vocabulary or concept of a particular news story.
- Play the broadcast again and have students complete the Radio News Broadcast Worksheet activity.
- Compare the students' answers and discuss why their perceptions of the story might be different.
- Repeat this activity for each news clip.

Evaluation: Students will be able to extract information from a radio news report.

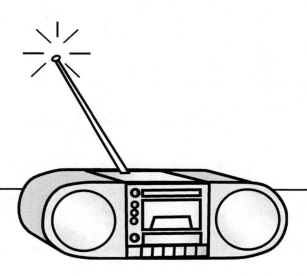

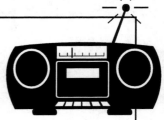

RADIO NEWS BROADCAST WORKSHEET

Name: _____

1. What is the general subject of the news report?

_____

2. Was it a local news item or a national news item?

_____

3. About how much time (in minutes or seconds) do you think was devoted to this story?

_____

4. Did you get a lot of information from the report?

_____

In the table below, please indicate the information you remember.

Who is the news about?	
What happened?	
Where did it occur?	
How did it happen?	
Why did it occur?	
Does it affect you? How?	
Is it good news or bad news?	

Do you feel you got a complete story from the radio news?

_____

Grade levels: 4–8

Standards: Language Arts, Thinking and Reasoning, Visual Arts

Activity description: Students will look at taped television news broadcasts on the same subjects as the previous activity done with radio broadcasts.

Preparation and materials:

- Tape several television news segments that have the same subject as the radio broadcasts in the previous activity.
    - ▶ Use at least one local and one national news segment.
- Copy a Television News Broadcast Worksheet for each student.

Procedure:

- Each student will have a Television News Broadcast Worksheet for each news clip.
- Play the first news broadcast for the class.
    - ▶ Go over any questions students might have concerning the vocabulary or concept of a particular news story.
- Play the broadcast again and have students complete the television news worksheet activity.
- Compare the students' answers and discuss why their perceptions of the story might be different.
- Repeat this activity for each news clip.

Evaluation: Students will be able to extract pertinent information from a television news broadcast.

TELEVISION NEWS BROADCAST WORKSHEET

Name: _____

1. What is the general subject of the news report?

    _____

2. Is it local or national news?

    _____

3. About how much time (in minutes or seconds) do you think was devoted to this story?

    _____

4. Did you get a lot of information from the report?

    _____

5. Who is the news about?_____

6. What happened?_____

7. Where did it occur?_____

8. Why did it happen?_____

9. Does it affect you? How?_____

10. Did the news commentator have an opinion about the story?_____

11. Did you get more information from the television or radio news?_____

12. Do you prefer listening to radio news or watching television news?_____

13. Indicate some reasons for your choice.

    _____

    _____

    _____

    _____

Grade levels: 4–8

Standards: Language Arts, Thinking and Reasoning, Working with Others

Activity description: The students will select appropriate jobs for themselves in order to create a school news program.

Preparation and materials:
- Tape player
- Whiteboard and chalkboard to record ideas

Procedure:
- The class will create a 15 minute news program to be aired over the school public address system.
- Brainstorm with the class to determine the different jobs involved in producing a radio news program, and what the specific qualifications for each might be.
    - *Presenter*
        - Can handle a microphone
        - Speaks clearly and has a pleasant speaking voice
    - *Interviewer*
        - Works with the team to develop questions
        - Asks the questions of the person being interviewed
    - *Note Taker/Transcriber*
        - Assists in an interview or at a scene by recording answers
        - Works with the team to develop questions
        - Can transcribe the interview to paper
    - *Technician*
        - Works with the team to develop questions
        - Is the person responsible for the care of the tape recorder and the recordings
        - Is the person responsible for the quality of the final show
        - Has some experience or is not fearful of electronic equipment
        - Can work quietly in the background
    - *Researcher*
        - Works with the team to develop questions
        - Does research for background information and current events
        - Likes to research and find information
    - *News Reporter*
        - Works with the research team to determine news content
        - Likes to write and is good at creating a news report
- Have students pick the jobs they want to do.

Evaluation: The students will select jobs that fit their specific likes and qualifications.

Activity 140 School Radio News Report

Grade levels: 4–8

Standards: Language Arts, Thinking and Reasoning, Working with Others

Activity description: Students will do the work required to create a news report.

Preparation and materials:
- Whiteboard or chalkboard for recording ideas

Procedure:
- The entire class will decide what news they want to present.
- Each report will be assigned a team.
- Each team will divide the work into the appropriate tasks.
- Students will begin the work by creating a plan for their report.
- Students will begin to collect necessary information.
- This activity can be ongoing for several days until each group is ready for a trial taping.
- When the groups are ready, deliver the news report over the school public address system.

Evaluation: Students in each group work together to create an informative news report.

Activity 141 The Fantasy Vacation: Travel Brochures

Grade levels: 4–8

Standards: Language Arts, Thinking and Reasoning, Visual Arts

Activity description: Students will examine travel brochures.

Preparation and materials:
- Collect travel brochures and display them in the classroom.

Procedure:
- Ask students to examine the travel brochures.
- Which vacations look the best?
- Ask students if they think the brochures are an honest representation of the actual vacation package.
- Analyze the media messages and clarify any misrepresentations for students.
- Have them determine what the target audience is for each brochure.

Evaluation: Students will understand that a travel brochure is a media message about a vacation package that is for sale.

Grade levels: 4–8

Standards: Language Arts, Thinking and Reasoning, Visual Arts, Geography

Activity description: The class will divide into groups and each group will gather information to create a travel brochure.

Preparation and materials:

- Whiteboard or chalkboard for recording ideas

- Internet access where possible for research

Procedure:

- Divide the class into groups.

- Each group will decide the destination of their travel brochure.

- Groups will distribute assignments.

  ▶ *Destination Coordinator* provides:
    - Detailed map of destination
    - Complete description of the area
    - Population and weather report
    - Languages spoken there
    - Holidays and religions
    - Government
    - Currency

  ▶ *Tour Guide* provides:
    - Specific areas of interest
    - A map and description of each area

  ▶ *Recreation Director* provides:
    - All types of indoor and outdoor activities
    - Maps, schedules, and prices of activities
    - Names and locations of restaurants and other recreation spots

  ▶ *Travel Agent* provides correct pricing for:
    - Transportation to destination
    - Transportation at the destination
    - Lodging
    - Meals

Evaluation: Students will work together and independently to gather necessary information.

Related Internet Resources:

Create a Travel Brochure: Mr. Kelly's Persuasive Writing Hot Links. 14 October 2003.
<http://www.beth.k12.pa.us/schools/wwwclass/kgrammes/kgwebquest/kgwebquest.htm>

Activity 143   Create a Travel Brochure II

Grade levels: 4–8

Standards: Language Arts, Thinking and Reasoning, Visual Arts, Geography

Activity description: Students will evaluate the information collected in the previous activity and create a travel brochure draft.

Preparation and materials:
- Provide students with paper that is the right size for a travel brochure.
- Allow time for Internet access to conduct research.

Procedure:
- Students will assemble and organize their information.
- Students will write rough drafts for the brochure.
- Each group will create a draft brochure, cutting and pasting pictures and articles.
  - ▶ Make sure groups emphasize the target audience!
- Students will exchange draft brochures for peer editing to see if each brochure is persuasive and effective. Students will make necessary changes.

Evaluation: Students will create a convincing and accurate travel brochure draft.

Activity 144   Get Ready and Go!

Grade levels: 4–8

Standards: Language Arts, Thinking and Reasoning, Visual Arts, Geography, Technology

Activity description: Students will create their final travel brochures.

Preparation and materials:
- Provide access to a word processing or desktop publishing program.

Procedure:
- Each group will create a travel brochure using either a word processing program or a desktop publishing program.
- Each brochure will require:
  - ▶ Pictures from the Internet
  - ▶ Good use of color and spacing
  - ▶ Logical organization of sections
  - ▶ Correct spelling and grammar
  - ▶ Accuracy of facts

Evaluation: Each group will create a travel brochure using a word processing or desktop publishing program.

Related Internet Resources:
Desktop Publishing Resources. *Travel Brochure Project*. 14 October 2003.
<http://www.geocities.com/CollegePark/Quad/5687/brochure.html>

Grade levels: 4–8

Standards: Language Arts, Thinking and Reasoning, Visual Arts

Activity description: Students will examine the wording on boxes of tissues and packages of toilet paper.

Preparation and materials:
- Purchase, bring to class, and display many different brands and types of tissues and toilet paper.
- You'll need a whiteboard or chalkboard to record answers.

Procedure:
- Group like items together.
- Students will examine each group.
- Students will note the terminology used in each one.
  - ▶ Is the tone different?
- What are the claims from the box?
- List the descriptive words used on each package.
- Have students consider whether the wording gets confusing.
- Ask them if they can really believe that one brand is softer or stronger than the other brand.
- Toilet paper comparisons:
  - ▶ List the adjectives on different brands
  - ▶ Is the paper advertised for number of sheets? Number of rolls? What is the difference?
  - ▶ Which one really offers the best value?

Evaluation: Students will recognize the vast array of products and the advertising tricks that are designed to get you to buy them.

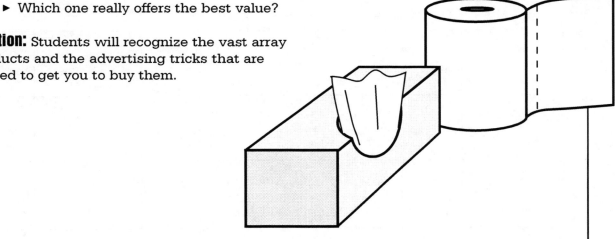

PRODUCT PACKAGE WORKSHEET

Name: _____

Examine the product packages carefully. Complete the worksheet.

Name of Product	Target Audience	Colors of Package	Information Available	Adjectives Used	Does It Appeal to You?

Activity 147　Reality Check

Grade levels: 4–8

Standards: Language Arts, Thinking and Reasoning, Visual Arts

Activity description: Students will be asked to determine whether a television character is real or not.

Preparation and materials:
- Collect several storybooks that have television characters in them.

Procedure:
- Read a story to the class.
- Ask class to identify the characters.
   - ▶ Are the characters real?
- Ask students what the difference is between a storybook character and a TV character.
- Ask them to explain why they think one character is real and the other isn't.

Evaluation: Students should be able to discern between a storybook character and a TV character.

Activity 148　Food!

Grade levels: 4–8

Standards: Language Arts, Thinking and Reasoning, Visual Arts

Activity description: Students will keep track of food commercials on television during a Saturday morning.

Preparation and materials:
- Assign students to watch one hour of television cartoons on a Saturday morning.

Procedure:
- Students will complete a Food and Television worksheet.

Evaluation: Students will become aware of the vast number of food commercials during children's programming.

FOOD AND TELEVISION

Name: _____

While you are watching TV on Saturday morning, watch carefully for food commercials. Please write the name of the show, the name of the product being advertised, and check if it is cereal or junk food.

Name of Product	TV Show	Cereal	Junk Food

Activity 150   Marketing Panel: Food

Grade levels: 4–8

Standards: Language Arts, Thinking and Reasoning, Visual Arts, Working with Others

Activity description: Students will learn how to evaluate products they see in advertisements.

Preparation and materials:
- Samples of foods that are advertised on morning television; several different brands of each are necessary;
  - ▶ Breakfast cereals
  - ▶ Juice
  - ▶ Sweets
- Chalkboard or whiteboard to record answers

Procedure:
- Divide students into groups to create several marketing panels.
- Select a group to go first.
- Give the students a sample portion of the first food. Do NOT reveal the brand of any of these foods.
- Students will tell you how it tastes and give you a one-word description for that food.
  - ▶ Record the answers.
- Proceed with other brands in the same food category.
- Have students vote on which tastes the best.
- Do the advertisements for this product convey the correct information?

Evaluation: Students will evaluate products for themselves.

Activity 151   Marketing Panel: Toy

Grade levels: 4–8

Standards: Language Arts, Thinking and Reasoning, Visual Arts, Working with Others

Activity description: Students will sample a new toy.

Preparation and materials:
- Acquire several toys that are advertised on television.
- Tape the ads for these toys.
- You'll need a whiteboard or chalkboard to record answers.

Procedure:
- Each market testing panel will get a Product Evaluation Worksheet to complete.
- Create a student panel to test market each toy.
- Show the students the toy advertisement.
- Discuss the expectations for the toy from the TV ad.
- Have students in each panel try the toy out and evaluate if it meets the expectations generated from the advertisement.

Evaluation: Students will understand that things are often misrepresented or exaggerated to sell the product.

PRODUCT EVALUATION WORKSHEET

Panel Members: _____

Name of toy: _____

Expectations from advertisement:

_____

_____

_____

_____

Results of testing toy:

_____

_____

_____

_____

Evaluation:

Did the toy meet your expectations?

_____

Did the advertisement portray the toy honestly?

_____

Activity 153 — Internet Advertising

Grade levels: 4–8

Standards: Language Arts, Thinking and Reasoning, Visual Arts, Technology

Activity description: Students will discuss the Internet and its food advertising and food portrayal.

Preparation and materials:
- Internet availability for class

Procedure:
- Direct the students to the Nabisco Company Web site.
  - ▶ NabiscoWorld.com <http://www.nabiscoworld.com/>
- Have them explore the different parts of the site.
- Discuss their findings.

Evaluation: Students will become aware that Internet games are often disguised advertisements.

Related Internet Resources:
Nabisco World. 1999–2003. KF Holdings. 19 October 2003. <http://www.nabiscoworld.com/>

Activity 154 — Television Advertising Strategies

Grade levels: 4–8

Standards: Language Arts, Thinking and Reasoning, Visual Arts

Activity description: Students will keep a record of TV ads during their evening viewing for four days (Mon.—Thurs.). They will return the Strategy Analysis worksheet on Friday and discuss the results.

Preparation and materials:
- Television Advertising Strategy worksheet for each student

Procedure:
- On a Monday, distribute the Television Advertising Strategy worksheet to your class.
- Discuss the terminology with the students so they are clear on the choices.
- Students will keep a record of TV ads from Monday through Thursday evenings and return the worksheet on Friday.
- On Friday, discuss the results with the class.

Evaluation: Students will be able to recognize the senses that advertising appeals to.

Related Internet Resources:
Center for Media Literacy. *Common Advertising Strategies.* 2001. 19 October 2003. <http://www.media-awareness.ca/english/resources/educational/handouts/advertising_marketing/common_ad_strats.cfm>

TELEVISION ADVERTISING STRATEGIES

Name: _____

While you watch a commercial on television, think of which category the ad falls into and indicate it on the worksheet.

Product Advertised	Ideal Kids	Heart Strings	Amazing Toys	Life-Like Settings	Sounds Good	Cute Celebrities	Selective Editing	Family Fun	Excitement	Star Power

Literature Connections: *Arthur's TV Trouble*

Grade levels: 4 and 5

Standards: Language Arts, Thinking and Reasoning, Visual Arts

Activity description: Read and discuss the book, *Arthur's TV Trouble*.

Preparation and materials:
- Obtain a copy of *Arthur's TV Trouble* by Marc Brown. Little Brown & Co. (Toronto, Canada), 1995.

Procedure:
- Read this story aloud to the children.
- Ask them if they have trouble resisting TV commercials like Arthur does.
- What kind of problems did not resisting commercials create in the story?
- How can problems be avoided?

Evaluation: Students will relate to Arthur and his TV commercial addiction.

Literature Connections: *The Bionic Bunny Show*

Grade levels: 4 and 5

Standards: Language Arts, Thinking and Reasoning, Visual Arts

Activity description: Read and discuss the book, *The Bionic Bunny Show*.

Preparation and materials:
- Obtain a copy of *The Bionic Bunny* Show by Marc Brown and Laurene Krasny Brown. Atlantic Monthly Press/Little Brown and Company (Boston, U.S.A.), 1984.
- You'll need a whiteboard or chalkboard to record responses.

Procedure:
- Read this story aloud to the children.
- Ask them if they have a TV super-hero.
- What kind of hero is it?
- Is the hero real?
- What do they think the hero is like when he or she isn't on television?

Evaluation: The book will help students to distinguish between fantasy and reality.

Activity 158 Literature Connections: Aunt Chip and the Great Triple Creek Dam Affair

Grade levels: 4 and 5

Standards: Language Arts, Thinking and Reasoning, Visual Arts

Activity description: Read and discuss the book, *Aunt Chip and the Great Triple Creek Dam Affair*.

Preparation and materials:
- Obtain a copy of *Aunt Chip and the Great Triple Creek Dam Affair* by Patricia Polacco. Philomel Books (New York, U.S.A.), 1996.
- You'll need a whiteboard or chalkboard to record responses.

Procedure:
- Read this story aloud to the children.
- Ask them if they think this could happen.
- Why did Aunt Chip go back to bed for 50 years?
- Did the town benefit from watching so much TV?
- Why did Aunt Chip believe in the power of books?

Evaluation: Students will understand the basic reasons to read.

Activity 159 Literature Connections: *Mouse TV*

Grade levels: 4 and 5

Standards: Language Arts, Thinking and Reasoning, Visual Arts

Activity description: Read and discuss the book, *Mouse TV.*

Preparation and materials:
- Obtain a copy of *Mouse TV* by Matt Novak. Orchard Books (New York, U.S.A.), 1994.
- You'll need a whiteboard or chalkboard to record responses.

Procedure:
- Read this story aloud to the children.
- Ask them if their TV has ever been broken.
- What did they do without the TV?
- Did the family relationships change when the TV broke?

Evaluation: Students will begin to understand the impact TV watching has on their lives.

Grade levels: 4 and 5

Standards: Language Arts, Thinking and Reasoning, Visual Arts

Activity description: Read and discuss the book, *Lyle at the Office*.

Preparation and materials:
- Obtain a copy of *Lyle at the Office* by Bernard Waber. Houghton Mifflin (Boston, USA), 1994.

Procedure:
- Read the story aloud to the class.
- Discuss the reasons Lyle is not allowed to be in a commercial to sell food.
- Ask students if they would they like to be in a commercial.
- What changes in lifestyle might occur after someone was in TV commercials?
- Was Lyle happy with his life without being on television?

Evaluation: Students will understand the impact fame has on someone's life.

Grade levels: 4–8

Standards: Language Arts, Thinking and Reasoning, Visual Arts

Activity description: Read and discuss the book, *The Wretched Stone*.

Preparation and materials:
- Obtain a copy of *The Wretched Stone* by Chris Van Allsberg. Houghton Mifflin (Boston, USA), 1991.

Procedure:
- Read the story aloud to the class.
- Discuss the appeal of the glowing rock.
- What affect did the glowing rock have on the crew of the Rita Anne?
- What changes occurred in the crew's lifestyle as they continued to gaze at the stone?
- What social skills did they lose?
- How did Mr. Howard help them return to normal?
- What are the comparisons to today?

Evaluation: Students will understand the affect television has on their lives.

Activity 162   Literature Connections: *Fix It*

Grade levels: 4 and 5

Standards: Language Arts, Thinking and Reasoning, Visual Arts

Activity description: Read and discuss the book, *Fix It*.

Preparation and materials:
- Obtain a copy of *Fix It* by David McPhail. Dutton Children's Books (New York, NY), 1984.

Procedure:
- Read the story aloud to the class.
- Why was Emma so upset?
- What kind of entertainment did Emma find to replace TV?
- What happened to Emma's interest in TV by the time the TV was fixed?

Evaluation: Students will get some additional options for entertainment other than TV.

Activity 163   Literature Connections: *Box-Head Boy*

Grade levels: 4–8

Standards: Language Arts, Thinking and Reasoning, Visual Arts

Activity description: Read and discuss the book, *The Box-Head Boy*.

Preparation and materials:
- Obtain a copy of *The Box-Head Boy* by Christine M. Winn. Fairview Press (Minneapolis, MN), 1996.

Procedure:
- Read the story aloud to the class.
- Have students brainstorm answers to the following questions:
    - What can happen to someone who watches too much TV?
    - What happens to Denny?
    - What limitations does Denny discover about the world of TV?

Evaluation: Students will consider the long-term affects of television watching.

Activity 164   Literature Connections: *Fred's TV*

Grade levels: 4–8

Standards: Language Arts, Thinking and Reasoning, Visual Arts

Activity description: Read and discuss the book, *Fred's TV.*

Preparation and materials:
- Obtain a copy of *Fred's TV* by Clive Dobson. Firefly Books (Willowdale, Canada), 1989.

Procedure:
- Read the story aloud to the class.
- What does Fred's father do to the TV?
- What does Fred do to solve his problem?
- What benefits did a broken TV eventually have for Fred?

Evaluation: Students will examine additional options for entertainment other than TV.

Activity 165   Literature Connections: *A Monster in My Mailbox*

Grade levels: 4–8

Standards: Language Arts, Thinking and Reasoning, Visual Arts

Activity description: Read and discuss the book, *A Monster in My Mailbox.*

Preparation and materials:
- Obtain a copy of *A Monster In My Mailbox* by Sheila Gordon. Clarke, Irwin and Company LTD. (Toronto, Canada), 1978.

Procedure:
- Read the story aloud to the class.
- Why is Julius disappointed with his monster?
- What options does Julius have for spending his money?
- What choices does he make?

Evaluation: Students will examine additional options for entertainment other than TV.

Activity 166   Literature Connections: *The Pinballs*

Grade levels: 4–8

Standards: Language Arts, Thinking and Reasoning, Visual Arts

Activity description: Read and discuss the book, *The Pinballs.*

Preparation and materials:
- Obtain a copy of *The Pinballs* by Betsy Byars. Fitzhenry and Whiteside Ltd. (Toronto, Canada), 1977.
- You'll need a whiteboard or chalkboard to record student answers.

Procedure:
- Assign the story to the class.
- What influences Carley's view of life more than anything else?
- Discuss Carley's lack of social skills.
    - ▶ What do you think caused them?

Evaluation: Students can learn how to care about themselves and each other from a model presented in the book.

Activity 167   Literature Connections: *Rosy Cole: She Walks in Beauty*

Grade levels: 4–8

Standards: Language Arts, Thinking and Reasoning, Visual Arts

Activity description: Read and discuss the book, *Rosy Cole: She Walks in Beauty*.

Preparation and materials:
- Obtain a copy of *Rosy Cole: She Walks in Beauty* by Sheila Greenwald. Little, Brown and Company (Toronto, Canada), 1994.
- You'll need a whiteboard or chalkboard to record answers.

Procedure
- Assign the story to the class.
- What influences do the media have on Rosy?
- Why does she want to get more attention?
- How does she plan on getting it?
- Does this make her happy?

Evaluation: Students will be offered a glimpse into someone obsessed with image and beauty.

Activity 168   Literature Connections: *The Secret Life of the Underwear Champ*

Grade levels: 4–8

Standards: Language Arts, Thinking and Reasoning, Visual Arts

Activity description: Read and discuss the book, *The Secret Life of the Underwear Champ*.

Preparation and materials:
- Obtain a copy of *The Secret Life of the Underwear Champ* by Betty Miles. Random House (Toronto, Canada), 1981.
- You'll need a whiteboard or chalkboard to record answers.

Procedure:
- Assign the story to the class.
- What is Larry's life missing that makes it different from a regular kid's life?
- What do photographers do to people that appear on television?
- What happens to change Larry's mind about modeling?

Evaluation: Students will see that famous people aren't always happiest.

Activity 169   Literature Connections: *Tom the Cat*

Grade levels: 4 and 5

Standards: Language Arts, Thinking and Reasoning, Visual Arts

Activity description: Read and discuss the book, *Tom the Cat*.

Preparation and materials:
- Obtain a copy of *Tom the Cat* by Joan Heibroner. Random House (New York, NY), 1994.
- You'll need a whiteboard or chalkboard to record answers.

Procedure:
- Read the story to the class.
- What is Tom trying to do?
- What happens to Tom?

Evaluation: Students will understand the difference between fantasy and reality.

Activity 170   Literature Connections: The Berenstain Bears and Too Much TV

Grade levels: 4 and 5

Standards: Language Arts, Thinking and Reasoning, Visual Arts

Activity description: Read and discuss the book, *The Berenstain Bears and Too Much TV*.

Preparation and materials:
- Obtain a copy of *The Berenstain Bears and Too Much TV* by Stan Berenstain and Jan Berenstain. Random House (New York, NY), 1984.
- You'll need a whiteboard or chalkboard to record answers.

Procedure:
- Read the story to the class.
- Why did Mama and Papa decide their children watched too much TV?
- What did they do to stop it?
- What happened to Brother and Sister Bear?

Evaluation: Students will realize that there are alternatives to watching TV.

Activity 171   Literature Connections: A Word from Our Sponsor, or My Friend Alfred

Grade levels: 4–8

Standards: Language Arts, Thinking and Reasoning

Activity description: Read and discuss the book, *A Word from Our Sponsor, or My Friend Alfred*.

Preparation and materials:
- Obtain a copy of *A Word from Our Sponsor, or My Friend Alfred* by Julie Angell. Bradbury Press (Scarsdale, NY), 1979.
- You'll need a whiteboard or chalkboard to record answers.

Procedure:
- Assign the story to the class.
- What is the problem in the story?
- Did Alfred do the right thing?
- How does this book explain the role of advertising?

Evaluation: Students will realize that they cannot always believe advertising.

Activity 172 — Literature Connections: *Television — What's Behind What You See*

Grade levels: 4–8

Standards: Language Arts, Thinking and Reasoning

Activity description: Read and discuss the book, *Television—What's Behind What You See.*

Preparation and materials:
- Obtain a copy of *Television—What's Behind What You See* by W. Carter Merbreier. Farrar, Strauss and Giroux (New York, NY), 1996.
- You'll need a whiteboard or chalkboard to record answers.

Procedure
- Read the story to the class.
- Discuss the elements of television production.
- Encourage students to ask questions about the different roles in creating a television show.

Evaluation: Students will be able to identify some of the behind-the-scenes activities that are part of a television production.

Activity 173 — Overcoming the Media Madness

Grade levels: 4–8

Standards: Language Arts, Visual Arts, Thinking and Reasoning, Working with Others

Activity description: Students will brainstorm ways to cut down the number of media messages they receive.

Preparation and materials:
- Chalkboard or whiteboard to record answers

Procedure:
- Ask students for some ideas to cut down on the media messages they receive.
- Record all answers.
- Discuss the effectiveness and possibility of each one with the class.
- Have the class select one idea and devise a plan to put it into action for the class.

Evaluation: Students will work together and agree on a plan to overcome media madness.

Activity 174   TV-Turnoff Week

Grade levels: 4–8

Standards: Language Arts, Visual Arts, Thinking and Reasoning, Working with Others

Activity description: Students will participate in the national TV-Turnoff Week.

Preparation and materials:
- Obtain literature and information on TV-Turnoff Week.

Procedure:
- Distribute the information to class and talk about the process.
- Students will return agreements before the week begins. These need to be signed by the whole family to encourage the completion of the activity.

Evaluation: Students will agree to turn off the TV for a week.

Related Internet Resources:
TV Turnoff Network. *TV-Turnoff Week*. 2001. 18 October 2003.
<http://www.tvturnoff.org/2003%20endorserssought.htm>

Activity 175   Activities without Television

Grade levels: 4–8

Standards: Language Arts, Visual Arts, Thinking and Reasoning, Working with Others

Activity description: Students will discuss what else they can do if they don't watch TV for a week.

Preparation and materials:
- Whiteboard or chalkboard to record answers

Procedure:
- Ask students what they might do if the TV was not available for a week.
- Record all answers.
- Discuss other possibilities.

Evaluation: Students may be surprised at the many things they can do instead of watching TV.

Related Internet Resources:
TV Turnoff Network. *101 Screen Free Activities*. 2001. 18 October 2003.
<http://www.tvturnoff.org/101.htm>

Activity 176 Take Action I

Grade levels: 4–8

Standards: Language Arts, Thinking and Reasoning, Working with Others

Activity description: Students will discuss media messages that might offend them.

Preparation and materials:
- Whiteboard or chalkboard to record information

Procedure:
- Discuss the possibility that a student might be offended or angered by a media message he or she received.
- Ask students if they ever feel this way.
- Encourage students to take action and voice their concerns.

Evaluation: Students will become aware that they have the ability to contact the author of the message and complain.

Related Internet Resources:
Media Awareness Network. *Voice Your Opinion*. 2002. 17 October 2003.
<http://www.media-awareness.ca/eng/med/home/diff/voice.htm#mags>

Activity 177 Take Action II

Grade levels: 4–8

Standards: Language Arts, Thinking and Reasoning, Working with Others

Activity description: Students will write letters to the appropriate parties to voice their concerns.

Preparation and materials:
- Whiteboard or chalkboard to record information

Procedure:
- Talk about the complaints the students have aired in previous activity.
- If possible, have class visit the *Media Awareness Network* Web site that explains the procedure step by step.
  - ► Voice Your Opinion! <http://www.media-awareness.ca/english/resources/ educational/handouts/ television_radio/voice_your_opinions.cfm>
    - This site offers sample letters and directions on who to contact for every possible media message!

Evaluation: Students will write letters if they have a concern about a media message.

Related Internet Resources:
Media Awareness Network. *Voice Your Opinion*. 2002. 17 October 2003.
<http://www.media-awareness.ca/english/resources/educational/handouts/ television_radio/voice_your_opinions.cfm>

Activity 178   Hold On To Your Money

Grade levels: 4–8

Standards: Thinking and Reasoning, Working with Others

Activity description: Discuss the economic impact an advertisement might have on your family.

Preparation and materials:
- Whiteboard or chalkboard to record answers

Procedure:
- Discuss the bottom line to all advertisements—selling a product or service.
  - How often do students ask someone to get them something they have seen on TV?
  - What kind of products are these?
  - How does advertising affect their families?
  - What can each person do to help the situation?
  - How often is the product something they really don't need or want?
  - If the product is purchased, does it always do what it says it will?

Evaluation: Students will come up with ideas to help stop buying things that are advertised.

Activity 179   Hold On To Your Money: Buy Nothing Day

Grade levels: 4–8

Standards: Thinking and Reasoning, Working with Others

Activity description: Students will discuss the concept of a "Buy Nothing Day."

Preparation and materials:
- Whiteboard or chalkboard to record answers
- Information on Buy Nothing Day (November 29 in the USA)

Procedure:
- Discuss the economic effects Buy Nothing Day would have.
- Ask students if it is possible for their families to participate in something like this.
- Offer students some background information on this British event.

Evaluation: Students might agree to plan their own Buy Nothing Day.

Related Internet Resources:
NOTE: This Web site is not for student viewing, but will give you good ideas to conduct this lesson.

Buy Nothing Day. 19 October 2003. <http://www.buynothingday.co.uk/index.html>

Adbusters. *Buy Nothing Day*. 18 October 2003. <http://adbusters.org/campaigns/bnd/>

Activity 180 — PBS Quiz

Grade levels: 4–8

Standards: Language Arts, Visual Arts, Thinking and Reasoning

Activity description: Students will take a quiz on media awareness.

Preparation and materials:
- Internet access or reproduction of this quiz for the class

Procedure:
- Offer students an opportunity to take this online quiz.
- Discuss the results and what they have learned in their media literacy lessons.

Evaluation: Students will be able to test their media awareness.

Related Internet Resources:
PBS Teacher Source. *Media Literacy Quiz.* 2002. 18 October 2003.
<http://www.pbs.org/teachersource/media_lit/quiz.shtm>

Activity 181 — Media Awareness: Kid's Corner

Grade levels: 4–8

Standards: Language Arts, Visual Arts, Thinking and Reasoning

Activity description: Students will visit an interactive Web site with media literacy activities.

Preparation and materials:
- Internet connection
- *Media Awareness Network* "Games For Kids" Web site section:
    - <http://www.media-awareness.ca/english/special_initiatives/games/index.cfm>

Procedure:
- Class will have an opportunity to explore this excellent Web site and have some fun, too!

Evaluation: Students will be exposed to media awareness options.

Related Internet Resources:
Media Awareness Network. *Just for Kids.* 18 October 2003.
<http://www.media-awareness.ca/english/special_initiatives/games/index.cfm>

Grade levels: 4–8

Standards: Language Arts, Visual Arts, Thinking and Reasoning, Working with Others

Activity description: Students will be asked to grade several advertisements.

Preparation and materials:
- Tape several television commercials that are age- and content-appropriate for your class.
- Make sure some of the commercials are exemplary, and select others that are not.

Procedure:
- Review the elements of a good advertisement with the class.
- Let the class create a rubric from 1 to 4, 4 being the highest quality, for each element of a commercial advertisement.
- Students will view advertisements, one at a time.
- After each one, ask students to deconstruct the ad and grade it on a scale of 1 to 4.
- Discuss their comments.

Evaluation: Students will demonstrate knowledge of the components of a good advertisement.

Additional Print Resources

Axelrod, Lauryn. *TV-Proof Your Kids*. Carol Publishing Group, 1997.

Axelrod examines the potentially damaging messages children learn from TV and offers excellent tips on how to expose the tricks, negative stereotypes and values, and violence in advertising.

Kornfield, Jack. *Buddha's Little Instruction Book*. Bantam Doubleday Dell Publishers, 1994.

A small handbook of Buddha's instructions, interpreted for contemporary life.

Levin, Diane E. *Remote Control Childhood? Combating the Hazards of Media Culture*. National Association for the Education of Young Children, 1998.

Some sections of this book discuss media culture and its effects on children, legal issues, research, how children experience the media, and taking action. Remaining sections deal mainly with classroom learning and community action.

Merbreier, W. Carter. *Television: What's Behind What You See*. Farrar, Straus and Giroux, 1996.

This book, designed for children, offers a look at the world of television production, with a behind-the-scenes look at cartoons, sitcoms, and other shows. The illustrations examine studios, station departments, satellites, and much more.

Additional Internet Resources for the Classroom Teacher

Alliance for a Media Literate America
<http://www.nmec.org/medialit.html>
Alliance for a Media Literate America is committed to promoting media literacy education that is focused on critical inquiry, learning, and skill-building rather than on media-bashing and blame.

Cable in the Classroom
<http://www.ciconline.com/default.htm>
In addition to great connections with curriculum and media, Cable in the Classroom offers fully developed units on media literacy. This is a must-see site.

Center for Media Literacy
<http://www.medialit.org/>
The Center for Media Literacy is dedicated to a new vision of literacy for the 21st century: the ability to communicate competently in all media forms. The site has resources, kits available for teachers, and links to other media literacy sites online.

Channel One Teacher
<http://www.teachworld.com/about/index.html>
Channel One Teacher.com has a mission statement to empower young people by keeping them informed of current events, by broadening their view of the world around them, by sharing stories about teenagers who have demonstrated the Power of One, and by teaching young people how the media works. The Web site contains activities, evaluation forms and lesson plans.

Curriculum Adventures
<http://www.studentactivities.com/index.htm>
This site contains some fabulous simulation exercises for cross-curricular activities and a list of excellent Internet links.

Education World Lesson Planning Article: It's News to Me. Teaching Kids About the Newspaper
<http://www.education-world.com/a_lesson/lesson140.shtml>
This site offers excellent ideas and excellent ideas and links for teaching the newspaper.

FAIR
<http://www.fair.org/whats-fair.html>
FAIR is the national media watch group that has been offering well-documented criticism of media bias and censorship since 1986. It works to invigorate the First Amendment by advocating for greater diversity in the press and by scrutinizing media practices that marginalize public interest, minority and dissenting viewpoints.

Media Awareness Network
<http://www.media-awareness.ca/>
This Canadian Web site offers practical support for media education in the home, school, and community with lesson plans, interactive Web-based activities, and sections for kids, educators, parents, and community members. The excellent and comprehensive activities make this one of the best choices to check out.

Mediachannel.org
<http://www.mediachannel.org/classroom/toolkit/>
A source for media news, this site also has a teacher's guide and a teacher's toolkit.

MediaLiteracy.com
<http://www.medialiteracy.com/whatismlpage.htm>
Medialiteracy.com has information and resources for media literacy education in the United States with links to non-U.S. sites. It includes activities for educators, parents, and children.

Media Literacy Clearinghouse
<http://www.med.sc.edu:1081/>
This is a Web site designed for K–12 educators who want to learn more about media literacy, integrate it into classroom instruction, and make their students more media aware. It is filled with links and resources.

Media Literacy Online Project—College of Education—University of Oregon—Eugene
<http://interact.uoregon.edu/MediaLit/HomePage>
An excellent resource of links relating to children and the Internet.

Media Literacy Project by Renee Hobbs
<http://www.reneehobbs.org/>
A comprehensive Web site with innovative curriculum ideas and articles about media literacy.

Media Literacy Resource Guide by Ontario Ministry of Education
<http://lilt.ilstu.edu/smexpos/what_is_media_literacy.htm>
This is an excellent introductory site to the concepts of media literacy. It contains main points, basic questions, and links. One of the links is an excellent glossary of media literacy terms.

Mid-Continent Research for Education and Learning—Media Literacy
<http://www.med.sc.edu:1081/mcrel.htm>
This incredible site is a compilation of content standards for K–12 curriculum in both searchable and browsable formats. This page in particular includes the categories in the McREL standards database which correlate to media literacy in the English/language arts, history, and media curriculum areas.

New Mexico Media Literacy Project
<http://www.nmmlp.org>
This is the site of the state of New Mexico's tremendous Media Literacy project to educate and inform its public and teachers. There are many excellent resources directly linked to this site.

Newspapers in Education (NIE)
<http://nieonline.com/>
Many newspapers have their own NIE sites with curriculum materials related to newspapers. This is the main NIE site and has fabulous links to lesson plans and other resources.

Ontario Media Literacy Home Page
<http://www.angelfire.com/ms/MediaLiteracy/index.html>
Ron DeBoer's Web site devoted to Media Literacy. The site includes benchmarks and activities for all grade levels and links to other sites.

Open Learning Agency—Instructional Materials in Media Literacy/Studies
<http://www.cln.org/subjects/media_inst.html>
This is an excellent collection of "theme pages" with curriculum links and lesson plans.

PBS Kids
<http://pbskids.org/dontbuyit/teachersguide.html>
The Public Broadcasting Station's exemplary Web site is devoted to educating our youth about the media. Including online activities and dozens of lesson plans, this is a resource you should bookmark.

Project Based Learning with Multimedia
<http://pblmm.k12.ca.us/index.html>
This site is composed by the San Mateo County Office of Education and has an overview, curriculum, sample classroom projects, and much more.

Project Look Sharp hosted by Ithaca State College
<http://www.ithaca.edu/looksharp/>
This is an Ithaca State College initiative to promote and support the integration of media literacy into all classroom curricula at all grade levels and instructional areas.

Utah Education Network Themepark
<http://www.uen.org/themepark/html/communication/media.html>
A site with many links to other media literacy sites about things to do, teacher resources, and educational programming.

Western Massachusetts Gender Equity Center. Lessons in Media Literacy and Gender Equity Curriculum
<http://www.genderequity.org/medialit/contents.html>
An excellent resource for lessons based on gender equity, directly connected to the Massachusetts standards.

Young Media Australia
<http://www.youngmedia.org.au/index.htm>
This site claims to be Australia's best source of up-to-date information about media and children for students, researchers, professionals, and parents and caregivers. Although it is Australia-based, the information is universal.

Index